RIGHTLY DIVIDING GOD'S WORD THROUGH DISPENSATIONS

RIGHTLY DIVIDING GOD'S WORD THROUGH DISPENSATIONS

VICTOR B. SHINGLER JR.

Copyright © 2006
Victor B. Shingler Jr.

All rights reserved. No part of this book may be reproduced in any form, except for the inclusion of brief quotations in a review, without permission in writing from the author or publisher.

ISBN: 978-1-890120-41-2

Library of Congress Control Number: 2006935303

Second Printing 2012

Printed in the United States by Morris Publishing®
3212 East Highway 30
Kearney, NE 68847
1-800-650-7888

Table of Contents

FOREWORD V
INTRODUCTION.. VII
1. DISPENSATION OF INNOCENCE..1
2. DISPENSATION OF CONSCIENCE 5
   IN THIS DISPENSATION: 7
3. DISPENSATION OF HUMAN GOVERNMENT 10
   IN THIS DISPENSATION: 13
4. THE DISPENSATION OF PROMISE 15
   IN THIS DISPENSATION: 18
5. DISPENSATION OF LAW 21
   IN THIS DISPENSATION: 22
6. DISPENSATION OF GRACE 26
   IN THIS DISPENSATION: 28
7. THE DISPENSATION OF JUDGMENT.................................30
   IN THIS DISPENSATION: 33
8. THE MILLENNIAL REIGN..34
   IN THIS DISPENSATION: 35
9. HOW DISPENSATIONS RELATE TO BOOKS OF THE BIBLE 37
10. CHURCH AGE DOCTRINE..45
    THE BAPTISM OF THE HOLY GHOST 45
    SALVATION 49
    ETERNAL SECURITY 53
    SIGNS 62
    THE RAPTURE 72
    THE JUDGMENT SEAT OF CHRIST 77
    THE SEVEN MYSTERIES 82
    PRIESTS 89
    ORDINANCES 92

11.	**THE KINGDOM OF GOD AND THE KINGDOM OF HEAVEN** 101	
	THE SERMON ON THE MOUNT 117	
	ABOUT THE KINGDOM OF GOD: 119	
12.	**DANIEL'S SEVENTY WEEKS** 121	
13.	**JOHN'S AND PETER'S BAPTISMS** 128	
14.	**THE GREAT WHITE THRONE JUDGMENT** 133	
15.	**CONCLUSION** 139	

Foreword

Authors Note: All scripture referenced and quoted within this book is from the King James Version of the Holy Bible. Any paraphrasing is duly noted within the text.

January 11, 1969 is a day that is firmly etched in my memory. It is the day I was saved. Since my father held the belief that a person should be in Church every time the doors were opened, you can imagine how many services I attended. The evening of January 11, my father decided we would go to a revival at a little Methodist Church across town from where we lived. At the invitation the Pastor walked over to where I was sitting and asked if I would like to be saved. I said I would and went to the altar. There I gave my heart to Jesus Christ. The following Easter Sunday I was baptized.

I spent the next seven years acting like I was saved only when I was in Church or around Church people with whom my parents associated. Every Sunday, Wednesday, and Thursday I went to Church, usually kicking and screaming. At age seventeen I told my father when I turned eighteen, I would never go back to Church and he could thank himself for that. His reply was, "When you turn eighteen you can do what you want, but until then you will do what I tell you to do." I have two words that I would like to say to my father if he could hear: "Thanks, dad."

I did get out of Church at eighteen and stayed out until I married my wife Cheryle, who also had been saved at an early age. God started dealing with us and we decided to attend Church.

We started to attend Church where my parents went and were getting fed. The problem then arose about questions that weren't getting answered. For example, I asked a Sunday School Teacher why tongues and healing weren't for today. The answer I received was, "Just because it isn't, that's why." I thought that was worse than no answer at all.

God knew my heart and knew I wanted to learn the Bible. He also knew that He was about to call me to teach His Word. What happened next was typical of the Lord. That old man, who dragged me to Church all those years, walked up to me at Church on Sunday morning and handed me a booklet. He said, "Have you ever seen this book, it is a good one." I took the booklet home and my wife read it first. She then read it out loud to me in between bursts of laughter. This booklet was entitled "Tongues, Signs, and Healing" by Dr. Peter S. Ruckman. In just a few pages this booklet explained why tongues, signs, and healing are not for today.

With this I realized that God had put the material out there through his men if I wanted to learn. Now, after twenty years of Bible study the Lord has taught me some things. I also realized if I had been taught the basics of dispensational truth when I first started back to Church, my Bible study would have been much more fruitful. The reason for this is that I wouldn't have wasted so much time wondering why some things were supposedly contradicted in the Bible.

The reason for this book is, hopefully God will use it to keep other Christians from going through what I went through. If you can understand dispensations you can rightly divide God's Word. These dispensations put people and doctrine in their proper places. I have attempted to explain these dispensations as simply as I can. My hope is God will use this feeble attempt at writing for His glory. Without Him we can do nothing.

Introduction

What is true Bible doctrine? Which religion or denomination is correct in its doctrine? How can you know?

Consider these questions:

1) Does anyone need a priest today? If so, where is the scripture to support this?
2) If someone claims to believe the "whole" Bible, why aren't they offering animal sacrifices?
3) Why do some observe the Sabbath and don't eat meat on certain days?
4) Why do some believe that baptism is necessary for salvation (called baptismal regeneration) while others believe it is one of the ordinances of the Church?
5) Are tongues, healing, and other signs for the Church today? If not, why not?
6) Can a Christian in the Church Age lose his salvation? If not, why not?
7) Are people saved the same way from Genesis to Revelation?
8) Is there a new birth involved in everyone's salvation from Genesis to Revelation?
9) At the stoning of Stephen did God wash His hands of Israel never to deal with them again?
10) Will the Church go through parts or all of the Great Tribulation? Will she be caught out before the start of the Great Tribulation?

There are Biblical answers to these questions and it doesn't have anything to do with who is right and who is wrong. It hinges on what the scriptures say. These scriptures are the King James Version of the Bible. If we prayerfully consider the questions and honestly want to know the truth, the Holy Spirit will give us light.

In this study we will focus first and foremost on doctrine. When we take this approach we most certainly will encounter those who disagree with us. These disagreements are the basis for all the different denominations and corrupt Bible versions on the market today.

When dealing with Bible doctrine certain questions need to be answered: Who is speaking? Of whom or what is being spoken? What element of time is involved or when did or when will the event take place? Without these questions being answered you cannot arrive at sound doctrine. In fact Satan will give you false doctrine:

(Gen. 3:1) "Yea, hath God said,"

People all over America are listening to so-called "teachers" and "preachers" and accepting everything they say as truth without ever checking them. Average Church members depend on their pastor or Bible teacher to keep them informed of issues concerning Bible doctrine. These same people are accountants, lawyers, doctors, and an endless list of professional people who are shrewd and careful when it comes to their income, retirement, family, and health. Put these same people in a Church and almost anything that goes on must be from God because it is in a Church, right? It isn't right. In fact it couldn't be more wrong. These people are being deceived by Satan.

God has put divisions in the Bible and He expects us to rightly divide:

> (2 Tim. 2:15) "Study to shew thyself approved unto God, a workman that needeth not to be ashamed, rightly dividing the word of truth."

When you don't rightly divide you place people in time settings where they don't belong. When this happens you develop doctrines of devils and damnable heresies.

> (1 Tim. 4:1) "Now the Spirit speaketh expressly, that in the latter times some shall depart from the faith, giving heed to seducing spirits, and doctrines of devils;"
>
> (2 Pet. 2:1) "But there were false prophets also among the people, even as there shall be false teachers among you, who privily shall bring in damnable heresies, even denying the Lord that brought them, and bring upon themselves swift destruction."

These divisions are called dispensations:

> (Eph. 1:10) "That in the dispensation of the fulness of times he might gather together in one all things in Christ, both which are in heaven, and which are on earth; even in him."

What defines these dispensational divisions is how God chooses to save people or dispense salvation at any given time. In the end man will have gone through eight different modes of salvation spanning some six thousand years of man's history. The outstanding characteristics common to all eight of these dispensations is they all end in man's failure to obey God.

Some people believe the whole Bible is doctrinally for everyone in every age. Some choose to believe the Bible in part. Some don't like what it says so they correct and adjust it to conform to their beliefs. To follow any of these methods of Bible interpretation is to commit spiritual suicide.

The dread of controversy should never be a determining factor in deciding doctrine. Jesus Christ Himself said He came to this earth to divide:

> (Luke 12:51) "Suppose ye that I am come to give peace on earth? I tell you, Nay; but rather division."

If your desire is to be doctrinally sound, you won't be popular:

> (Matt 6:24) "No man can serve two masters: for either he will hate the one, and love the other; or else he will hold to the one, and despise the other. Ye cannot serve God and mammon."

Human nature tells a person that nothing good or worthwhile comes free. When people come under the conviction of the Holy Spirit and trust Jesus Christ, He saves their soul. Therefore, they have nothing as far as works are concerned in their salvation.

> (Eph. 2:8-9) "For by grace are ye saved through faith; and that not of yourselves: it is the gift of God: Not of works, lest any man should boast."

The old nature, which is still present,

(Rom. 7:14-18) "For we know that the law is spiritual: but I am carnal, sold under sin. For that which I do I allow not: for what I would, that do I not; but what I hate, that do I. If then I do that which I would not, I consent unto the law that it is good. Now then it is no more I that do it, but sin that dwelleth in me. For I know that in me (that is, in my flesh.) dwelleth no good thing: for to will is present with me; but how to perform that which is good I find not."

coupled with the influence of Satan, convinces the Christian that he has to work to be saved, regardless of what the scripture says. You cannot interpret scripture in light of your feelings. You have to interpret your feelings in light of scripture.

1. Dispensation of Innocence

The dispensation is entitled innocence because Adam and Eve didn't have knowledge of good and evil.

Length of this dispensation: unknown

Beginning: The creation of man.

> (Gen. 1:27) "So God created man in his own image, in the image of God created he him; male and female created he them."

Ending: The fall of man.

> (Gen. 3:23) "Therefore the Lord God sent him forth from the garden of Eden, to till the ground from whence he was taken."

Man's responsibility: To dress the garden, eat of the garden, and do not eat of the tree of knowledge of good and evil.

> (Gen. 2:15-17) "And the Lord God took the man, and put him into the garden of Eden to dress it and to keep it. And the Lord God commanded the man, saying, Of every tree of the garden thou mayest freely eat: But of the tree of the knowledge of good and evil, thou shalt not eat of it: for in the day that thou eatest thereof thou shalt surely die."

Man's failure: He was innocent of the knowledge of good and evil and disobeyed God and ate of the tree of knowledge of good and evil.

> (Gen. 3:12) "And the man said, The woman whom thou gavest to be with me, she gave me of the tree, and I did eat."

The Judgment: Adam and Eve were sent out of the garden. The woman was to be in subjection. The man was then made to farm the land for his food.

> (Gen 3:16) "Unto the woman he said, I will greatly multiply thy sorrow and thy conception; in sorrow thou shalt bring forth children; and thy desire shall be to thy husband, and he shall rule over thee."
> (Gen. 3:23) "Therefore the Lord God sent him forth from the garden of Eden, to till the ground from whence he was taken."

Salvation: Works with no new birth or indwelling of the Holy Spirit.

Object of God's dealing: The first couple, Adam and Eve.

IN THIS DISPENSATION:

Adam named every creature God created.

> (Gen. 2:19) "And out of the ground the Lord God formed every beast of the field, and every fowl of the air; and brought them unto Adam to see what he would call them: and

> whatsoever Adam called every living creature, that was the name thereof."

The serpent tricked Eve into eating of the tree of knowledge of good and evil by putting doubt in her mind of God's Word.

> (Gen. 3:1-5) "Now the serpent was more subtil than any beast of the field which the Lord God had made. And he said unto the woman, Yea hath God said, Ye shall not eat of every tree of the garden? And the woman said unto the serpent, We may eat of the fruit of the trees of the garden: But of the fruit of the tree which is in the midst of the garden, God hath said, Ye shall not eat of it, neither shall ye touch it, lest ye die. And the serpent said unto the woman, Ye shall not surely die: For God doth know that in the day ye eat thereof, then your eyes shall be opened, and ye shall be as gods, knowing good and evil."

Eve ate and gave to Adam who ate also.

> (Gen. 3:6) "And when the woman saw that the tree was good for food, and that it was pleasant to the eyes, and a tree to be desired to make one wise, she took of the fruit thereof, and did eat, and gave also unto her husband with her; and he did eat."

At this point they both were enlightened and no longer innocent. Realizing themselves to be naked they sewed fig leaves together to make clothes and covered themselves.

> (Gen. 3:7) "And the eyes of them both were opened, and they knew that they were naked; and they sewed fig leaves together, and made themselves aprons."

God placed Cherubims east of the Garden of Eden and a flaming sword which turned every way to keep the way of the tree of life. This, He did because He couldn't let fallen man live forever in this sinful state.

> (Gen 3:24) "So he drove out the man; and he placed at the east of the garden of Eden Cherubims, and a flaming sword which turned everyway, to keep the way of the tree of life."

2. Dispensation of Conscience

This dispensation is called conscience because upon eating of the tree of knowledge Adam and Eve became aware of what was good and what was evil. This was then passed on to the whole human race through them. God then gave man the opportunity to keep himself pure through his conscience.

Length of this dispensation: 1656 years.

Beginning: The fall of man.

> (Gen. 3:23) "Therefore the Lord God sent him forth from the garden of Eden, to till the ground from whence he was taken."

Ending: Noah's Flood

> (Gen. 8:15-17) "And God spake unto Noah, saying, Go forth of the ark, thou and thy wife, and thy sons, and thy son's wives with thee. Bring forth with thee every living thing that is with thee, of all flesh, both of fowl, and of cattle, and of every creeping thing that creepeth upon the earth; that they may breed abundantly in the earth, and be fruitful, and multiply upon the earth."

Man's responsibility: To give heed to three witnesses:

1) Man's own conscience.
2) The natural creation.
3) God Himself.

> (Gen. 6:5) "And God saw that the wickedness of man was great in the earth, and that every imagination of the thoughts of his heart was only evil continually."

Man's failure: To keep his generations pure through his conscience.

> (Gen. 6:5)

Man was wicked to his very core and the witness of God and nature was not enough to keep him from sinning.

> (Gen. 6:5)

The Judgment: A worldwide flood that destroyed all living creatures that were on the face of the earth.

> (Gen. 6:17) "And, behold, I, even I, do bring a flood of waters upon the earth, to destroy all flesh, wherein is the breath of life, from under heaven; and every thing that is in the earth shall die."

Salvation: Works with no new birth or indwelling of the Holy Spirit.

Object of God's dealing: The human race.

IN THIS DISPENSATION:

Eve had twin sons: Cain and Abel.

> (Gen. 4:1-2) "And Adam knew Eve his wife; and she conceived, and bare Cain, and said, I have gotten a man from the Lord. And she again bare his brother Abel. And Abel was a keeper of sheep, but Cain was a tiller of the ground."

Cain brought a sacrifice to God, which was the wrong sacrifice, and God rejected him for it. This made him angry enough to murder his brother who had brought the correct sacrifice.

> (Gen. 4:3-8) "And in process of time it came to pass, that Cain brought of the fruit of the ground an offering unto the Lord. And Abel, he also brought of the firstlings of his flock and of the fat thereof. And the Lord had respect unto Abel and to his offering: but unto Cain and to his offering he had not respect. And Cain was very wroth, and his countenance fell. And the Lord said unto Cain, why art thou wroth? And why is thy countenance fallen? If thou doest well, shalt thou not be accepted? And if thou doest not well, sin lieth at the door. And unto thee shall be his desire, and thou shalt rule over him. And Cain talked with Abel his brother: and it came to pass, when they were in the field, that Cain rose up against Abel his brother, and slew him."

For this, God cursed Cain and set a mark on him so no one would kill him.

> (Gen. 4:11) "And now thou art cursed from the earth, which hath opened her mouth to receive thy brother's blood from thy hand."
> (Gen. 4:15) "And the Lord said unto him, Therefore whosoever slayeth Cain, vengeance shall be taken on him sevenfold. And the Lord set a mark upon Cain, lest any finding him should kill him."

The first man who ever lived, died.

> (Gen. 5:5) "And all the days that Adam lived were nine hundred and thirty years: and he died."

Enoch was taken alive or raptured into heaven.

> (Gen. 5:24) "And Enoch walked with God: and he was not; for God took him."

Noah was given dimensions and orders to build the ark.

> (Gen. 6:14-16) "Make thee an ark of Gopher wood; rooms shalt thou make in the ark, and shalt pitch it within and without with pitch. And this is the fashion which thou shalt make it of: the length of the ark shall be three hundred cubits, the breadth of it fifty cubits, and the height of it thirty cubits. A window shalt thou make to the ark, and in a cubit shalt thou finish it above; and the door of the ark shalt thou set in the side thereof;

with lower, second, and third stories shalt thou make it."

Noah was commanded by God to enter the ark with his wife, sons, son's wives and enough animals to repopulate the earth.

(Gen. 7:7-9) "And Noah went in, and his sons, and his wife, and his son's wives with him, into the ark, because of the waters of the flood. Of clean beasts, and of beasts that are not clean, and of fowls, and of everything that creepeth upon the earth. There went in two and two unto Noah into the ark, the male and the female as God had commanded Noah."

The flood came and destroyed all living things on the face of the earth:

(Gen. 6:17) "And, behold, I, even I, do bring a flood of waters upon the earth, to destroy all flesh, wherein is the breath of life, from under heaven: and every thing that is in the earth shall die."

3. Dispensation of Human Government

This dispensation is called Human Government because people were to govern themselves.

Length of this dispensation: 427 years.

Beginning: Noah, his family, and the animals exiting the ark to replenish the earth.

> (Gen. 8:15-19) "And God spake unto Noah, saying, go forth of the ark, thou, and thy wife, and thy sons, and thy son's wives with thee. Bring forth with thee every living thing that is with thee, of all flesh, both of fowl, and of cattle, and of every creeping thing that creepeth upon the earth; that they may breed abundantly in the earth, and be fruitful, and multiply upon the earth. And Noah went forth, and his sons, and his wife, and his son's wives with him: Every beast, every creeping thing, and every fowl, and whatsoever creepeth upon the earth, after their kinds, went forth out of the ark."

Ending: God calling Abraham out of his homeland and moving him to the Promised Land.

(Gen. 12:1) "Now the Lord had said unto Abram, get thee out of thy country, and from thy kindred and from thy father's house, unto a land that I will shew thee."

Man's responsibility: To govern or police himself.

(Gen. 9:5-7) "And surely your blood of your lives will I require; at the hand of every beast will I require it, and at the hand of man; at the hand of every man's brother will I require the life of man. Who so sheddeth man's blood, by man shall his blood be shed: for in the image of God made he man. And you, be ye fruitful, and multiply; bring forth abundantly in the earth, and multiply therein."

Man's failure: he didn't worship God and tried to unite to make for himself a name.

(Gen. 11:4-6) "And they said, go to let us build us a city and a tower, whose top may reach unto heaven; and let us make us a name, lest we be scattered abroad upon the face of the whole earth. And the Lord came down to see the city and the tower, which the children of men builded. And the Lord said, behold, the people is one, and they have all one language; and this they begin to do: and now nothing will be restrained from them, which they have imagined to do."

The Judgment: The confounding of the language and scattering the people.

(Gen. 11:7-9) "Go to, let us go down, and there confound their language that they may not understand one another's speech. So the Lord scattered them abroad from thence upon the face of all the earth: and they left off to build the city. Therefore is the name of it called Babel; because the Lord did there confound the language of all the earth: and from thence did the Lord scatter them abroad upon the face of all the earth."

Salvation: Grace through faith with no new birth or indwelling of the Holy Spirit.

Object of God's dealing: The human race as a whole.

IN THIS DISPENSATION:

God promised to never destroy the earth again by water and gave the rainbow as a reminder of this:

> (Gen. 9:12-16) "And God said, this is the token of the covenant which I make between me and you and every living creature that is with you, for perpetual generations: I do set my bow in the cloud, and it shall be for a token of a covenant between me and the earth. And it shall come to pass, when I bring a cloud over the earth, that the bow shall be seen in the cloud: And I will remember my covenant, which is between me and you and every living creature of all flesh; and the waters shall no more become a flood to destroy all flesh. And the bow shall be in the cloud: and I will look upon it, that I may remember the everlasting covenant between God and every living creature of all flesh that is upon the earth."

Noah grew some grapes and drank of the fermented juice. With Noah in a drunken stupor his oldest son committed an act of sodomy on his father while the old man lay passed out and naked in his tent. This brought a curse on Ham's descendants:

> (Gen. 9:20-25) "And Noah began to be a husbandman, and he planted a vineyard: And he drank of the wine, and was drunken; and he was uncovered within his tent. And Ham, the father of Canaan, saw the

nakedness of his father, and told his two brethren without. And Shem and Japeth took a garment, and laid it upon both their shoulders, and went backward, and covered the nakedness of their father; and their faces were backward, and they saw not their father's nakedness. And Noah awoke from his wine, and knew what his younger son had done unto him. And he said, cursed be Canaan; a servant of servants shall he be unto his brethren."

The earth became of one language.

(Gen. 11:1) "And the whole earth was of one language, and of one speech."

4. The Dispensation of Promise

This dispensation is called Promise because of the promise God made to Abram:

> (Gen. 15:18) "In the same day the Lord made a covenant with Abram, saying, Unto thy seed have I given this land, from the river of Egypt unto the great river, the river Euphrates."

Length of dispensation: About 430 years.

Beginning: God called Abram out of his homeland.

> (Gen. 12:1) "Now the Lord had said unto Abram, Get thee out of thy country, and from thy kindred, and from thy father's house, unto a land that I will shew thee."

Ending: God gave Israel the law after he had delivered them out of Egypt:

> (Exo. 20:1-17) "And God spake all these words, saying...Thou shalt not covet thy neighbor's house, thou shalt not covet thy neighbor's wife, nor his manservant, nor his maidservant, nor his ox, nor his ass, nor anything that is thy neighbors."

Man's responsibility: Three things

Do sacrifice to God:

> (Gen. 15:9-10, 17) "And he said unto him, take me an heifer of three years old, and a she goat of three years old, a ram of three years old, and a turtledove, and a young pigeon. And he took unto him all these, and divided them in the midst, and laid each piece one against another: but the birds divided he not."
>
> (vs. 17) "And it came to pass, that when the sun went down, and it was dark, behold a smoking furnace, and a burning lamp that passed between those pieces."

Circumcision:

> (Gen. 17:9-14) "And God said unto Abraham, Thou shalt keep my covenant therefore, thou and thy seed after thee in their generations. This is my covenant which ye shall keep, between me and you and thy seed after thee; every man child among you shall be circumcised... And the uncircumcised man child whose flesh of his foreskin is not circumcised, that soul shall be cut off from his people; he hath broken my covenant."

Stay in the Land:

> (Gen. 24:7) "The Lord God of heaven, which took me from my father's house, and from the land of my kindred, and which

> spake unto me, and that swear unto me, saying, Unto thy seed will I give this land; he shall send his angel before thee, and thou shalt take a wife unto my son from thence."

Man's failure: The heathen got worse rather than repent and turned to idolatry:

> (Gen. 19:13) "For we will destroy this place, because the cry of them is waxen great before the face of the Lord; and the Lord hath sent us to destroy it."
> (Gen. 31:19) "And Laban went to shear his sheep: and Rachel had stolen the images that were her father's."
> (Exo. 12:12) "For I will pass through the land of Egypt this night, and will smite all the first born in the land of Egypt, both man and beast; and against all the gods of Egypt I will execute judgment: I am the Lord."

The Judgment: Israel, in bondage, in Egypt.

> (Exo. 1:14) "And they made their lives bitter with hard bondage in mortar, and in brick, and in all manner of service in the field: all their service, wherein they made them serve, was with rigor."

Salvation: Grace through faith with no new birth or permanent indwelling of the Holy Spirit.

Object of God's dealing: Abraham and his family.

IN THIS DISPENSATION:

You find the destruction of Sodom and Gomorrah.

(Gen. 19:24-25) "Then the Lord rained upon Sodom and upon Gomorrah brimstone and fire from the Lord out of heaven; And he overthrew those cities, and all the plain, and all the inhabitants of the cities, and that which grew upon the ground."

The Lord instructed Abraham to sacrifice Isaac:

(Gen. 22:2) "And he said, Take now thy son, thine only son Isaac, whom thou lovest, and get thee into the land of Moriah; and offer him there for a burnt offering upon one of the mountains which I will tell thee of."

Isaac marries Rebekah:

(Gen. 24:67) "And Isaac brought her into his mother Sarah's tent, and took Rebekah, and she became his wife; and he loved her: and Isaac was comforted after his mother's death."

Joseph rises to power in Egypt:

(Gen. 41:41) "And Pharaoh said unto Joseph, see, I have set thee over all the land of Egypt."

Moses is born, is miraculously allowed to live, and reared by his mother:

> (Exo. 1:15-16) "And the king of Egypt spake to the Hebrew midwives, ...And he said, When ye do the office of a midwife to the Hebrew women, and see them upon the stools; if it be a son, then ye shall kill him: but if it be a daughter, then she shall live."
>
> (Exo. 2:2) "And the woman conceived, and bare a son: and when she saw him that he was a goodly child, she hid him three months."
>
> (Exo 2:8,9) "And Pharaoh's daughter said to her, Go, and the maid went and called the child's mother. And Pharaoh's daughter said unto her, Take this child away, and nurse it for me, and I will give thee thy wages. And the woman took the child, and nursed it."

God calls Moses to lead the Children of Israel out of Egypt:

> (Exo. 3:10) "Come now therefore, and I will send thee unto Pharaoh, that thou mayest bring forth my people the children of Israel out of Egypt."

Moses opposes Pharaoh:

> (Exo.3:10-12:31) "Come now therefore ...And he called for Moses and Aaron by night, and said, Rise up, and get you forth from among my people, both ye and the

children of Israel; and go, serve the Lord, as ye have said."

First sickness and first healing recorded:

(Exo. 4:6-7) "And the Lord said furthermore unto him, Put now thine hand into thy bosom. And he put his hand into his bosom: and when he took it out, behold, his hand was leprous as snow. And he said, Put thine hand into thy bosom again. And he put his hand into his bosom again: and plucked it out of his bosom, and behold, it was turned again as his other flesh."

God parts the Red Sea:

(Exo. 14:21-22) "And Moses stretched out his hand over the sea; and the Lord caused the sea to go back by a strong east wind all that night, and made the sea dry land, and the waters were divided. And the children of Israel went into the midst of the sea upon the dry ground: and the waters were a wall unto them on their right hand, and on their left."

5. Dispensation of Law

This dispensation is called Law because the Nation of Israel is given the Mosaic Law to follow.

Length of dispensation: About 1491 years.

Beginning: The giving of the law.

> (Exo. 20:1-17) "And God spake all these words, saying ...Thou shalt not covet thy neighbor's house, Thou shalt not covet thy neighbor's wife, nor his manservant, nor his maidservant, nor his ox, nor his ass, nor anything that is thy neighbor's."

Ending: The birth of Christ.

> (Matt. 1:18) "Now the birth of Jesus Christ was on this wise."

Man's responsibility: Abide by the law and offer sacrifices for sin.

Man's failure: The rejection of the written and Incarnate Word.

> (Mark 7:9) "And he said unto them, full well ye reject the commandment of God, that ye may keep your own tradition."

> (Matt. 20:19) "And shall deliver him to the Gentiles to mock, and to scourge, and to crucify him: and the third day he shall rise again."

The Judgment: The Jew went into apostasy and captivity.

> (Rom. 10:21) "But to Israel he saith, all day long I have stretched forth my hands unto a disobedient and gainsaying people."
>
> (Dan. 9:24) "Seventy weeks are determined upon thy people and upon thy holy city, to finish the transgression, and to make an end of sins, and to make reconciliation for iniquity, and to bring in everlasting righteousness, and to seal up the vision and prophecy, and to anoint the most Holy."

Salvation: Faith and works under grace with no new birth or permanent indwelling of the Holy Spirit.

Object of God's dealing: Israel as a nation.

IN THIS DISPENSATION:

Saul, David and Solomon each reigned 40 years.

David slew Goliath:

> (1 Sam. 17:50) "So David prevailed over the Philistine with a sling and with a stone, and

smote the Philistine, and slew him; but *there* was no sword in the hand of David"

David and Bathsheba:

(2 Sam. 11:2-27) "And it came to pass in an eveningtide, that David arose from off his bed, and walked upon the roof of the king's house: and from the roof he saw a woman washing herself; and the woman was very beautiful to look upon... And David sent messengers, and took her; and she came in unto him, and he lay with her; for she was purified from her uncleanness: and she returned unto her house... David sent and fetched her to his house, and she became his wife, and bare him a son. But the thing that David had done displeased the Lord."

This dispensation includes all the times of the Kings of Israel and Judah. This is found in First Kings, Second Kings, First Chronicles, and Second Chronicles. It includes all the prophets from Isaiah to Malachi. It includes all four gospels up to Jesus Christ's death, thus recording the times of His life.

This dispensation introduces the signs to the nation of Israel. The first time a man gets sick:

(Exo. 4:6) "And the Lord said furthermore unto him, Put now thine hand into thy bosom. And he put his hand into his bosom: and when he took it out, behold, his hand was leprous as snow."

The first healing that ever took place.

> (Exo. 4:7) "And he said, Put thine hand into thy bosom again. And he put his hand into his bosom again; and plucked it out of his bosom: and, behold, it was turned again as his other flesh."

The Nation of Israel requires a sign and will get a sign when God is dealing with Jews.

> (1 Cor. 1:22) "For the Jews require a sign."

Between the Dispensations of Law and Grace there is a time of change. These changes occur because God was closing the Old Testament and opening the New Testament. Also God was going to stop dealing with the Nation of Israel and start dealing with people of all races, kindreds, and tongues on an individual basis. This time of change is called a transitional period.

God knew man would need guidance during this period of transition. He gave this guidance through the Books of Matthew and Acts. Matthew made the transition between the Old Testament and the New Testament. The Book of Acts covered the transition between the Nation of Israel and the Church.

These two transitional books are spiritual death traps for some Christians. They get bogged down trying to make application of the doctrine in these transitional books to themselves and other Christians. The doctrine contained in Matthew can be applied to the transition between the Testaments. Matthew also has doctrine for the Tribulation (Matt. 24,25) and the Millennium (Matt. 5,6,7). The Book of Acts contains the doctrine for the transition between the Jews and the Church. This transition takes place from Acts

1 to Acts 14. From Acts 15 to Acts 28 you are doctrinally in the Church age.

Rightly dividing (2 Tim. 2:15) are the two words that need to be exercised when dealing with the Books of Matthew and Acts 1-14. There is so little that can be doctrinally applied to a Church Age Christian. After knowing that you are saved by grace through faith why apply doctrine to yourself that includes works for salvation?

The only honest answer to this question that makes sense is: you don't believe Christ's blood sacrifice on the cross is enough to save you or keep you. If Satan can convince you that works are needed to get saved or stay saved, he has you where he wants you. He will worry you about working to stay saved when you should be working because you are saved. You would be well advised to stay out of that mess. This subject will be addressed in more detail in Chapter 10.

6. Dispensation of Grace

This dispensation is called grace because you are saved by grace through faith.

Length of this dispensation 2000 years?

Beginning: Acts with the disputation on circumcision:

> (Acts 15:1-2) "And certain men which came down from Judea taught the brethren, *and said*, except ye be circumcised after the manner of Moses, ye cannot be saved. When therefore Paul and Barnabas had no small dissention and disputation with them, they determined that Paul and Barnabas, and certain other of them, should go up to Jerusalem unto the apostles and elders about this question."
> (Acts 15:11) "But we believe that through the grace of the Lord Jesus Christ we shall be saved, even as they."

Ending: The calling out or rapture of the body of Christ or the Church.

> (1 Thes. 4:16-17) "For the Lord himself shall descend from heaven with a shout, with the voice of the archangel, and with the trump of God: and the dead in Christ shall rise first: Then we which are alive and

remain shall be caught up together with them in the clouds, to meet the Lord in the air: and so shall we ever be with the Lord."

Man's responsibility: Trust the sinless Son of God for the sacrifice He made on the cross.

(Eph. 5:2) "And walk in love, as Christ also hath loved us, and hath given himself for us an offering and a sacrifice to God for a sweet smelling savour."

Man's failure: Rejection of the Gospel of Jesus Christ and the Church goes into apostasy:

(Acts. 26:28) "Then Agrippa said unto Paul, almost thou persuadest me to be a Christian."
(2 Thes. 2:3) "Let no man deceive you by any means: for that day shall not come, except there come a falling away first, and that man of sin be revealed, the son of perdition"

The Judgment: Church will be caught out or raptured:

(Rev. 4:1) "After this I looked, and, behold, a door was opened in heaven: and the first voice which I heard was as it were of a trumpet talking with me; which said, come up hither, and I will shew thee things which must be hereafter."

Salvation: Grace through faith with a new birth and the permanent indwelling of the Holy Spirit.

(Eph. 2:8-9) "For by grace are ye saved through faith; and that not of yourselves: it is the gift of God: not of works, lest any man should boast."

(1 Pet. 1:23) "Being born again, not of corruptible seed, but of incorruptible, by the word of God, which liveth and abideth forever."

(2 Tim. 1:14) "That good thing which was committed unto thee keep by the Holy Ghost which dwelleth in us."

Object of God's dealing: Individuals, mainly Gentiles.

(Rom. 11:11) "I say then, Have they stumbled that they should fall? God forbid: but rather through their fall salvation is come unto the Gentiles, for to provoke them to jealousy."

IN THIS DISPENSATION:

Is the following:

1) The completion of the New Testament scriptures.
2) The Apostles being beaten and killed for the sake of the Gospel.
3) Christians being persecuted and killed by the Roman Catholic Church.
4) Millions of Jews being killed by Germany and Russia.
5) Israel becoming a nation again in 1948.

6) The preaching of men like Billy Sunday, Dwight L. Moody, Bob Jones Sr., Charles Spurgeon, and many others like them.
7) The translation of the A.V. 1611 King James Version.
8) The Body of Christ or Church going into total apostasy so that you can't distinguish between it and the world.

Between the Church Age and The Great Tribulation Period will be another transitional period. This period makes the transition from the Church back to the Nation of Israel. It moves from salvation through faith to faith and works. This transition is covered in the Book of Hebrews.

In Hebrews people can lose their salvation. After losing their salvation it is impossible to be saved again. This is another Book that a Church Age Christian should stay away from doctrinally. The title of the Book itself should tell you this. You are not a Hebrew.

7. The Dispensation of Judgment

This dispensation is called Judgment because God will judge Israel, The Roman Catholic Church and the nations on earth. The Church will be judged in heaven.

Length of this dispensation: 7 years.

Beginning: After the Rapture of the Church, probably immediately after.

> (Rev. 4:1) "After this I looked, and, behold, a door was opened in heaven: and the first voice which I heard was as it were of a trumpet talking with me; which said, Come up hither, and I will shew thee things which must be hereafter."

Ending: The Second Advent of Jesus Christ.

> (Rev. 19:11-15) "And I saw heaven opened, and behold a white horse; and he that sat upon him was called Faithful and True, and in righteousness he doth judge and make war. His eyes were as a flame of fire, and on his head were many crowns; and he had a name written, that no man knew, but he himself. And he was clothed with a vesture dipped in blood: and his name is called The Word of God. And the armies which were in heaven followed him upon white horses,

> clothed in fine linen, white and clean. And out of his mouth goeth a sharp sword, that with it he should smite the nations: and he shall rule them with a rod of iron: and he treadeth the winepress of the fierceness and wrath of Almighty God."

Man's responsibility: Keep the Commandments of God, have the testimony of Jesus Christ, and do not take the Mark of the Beast.

> (Rev. 12:17) "And the dragon was wroth with the woman, and went to make war with the remnant of her seed, which keep the Commandments of God, and have the testimony of Jesus Christ."
> (Rev. 13:18) "Here is wisdom. Let him that hath understanding count the number of the beast: for it is the number of a man; and his number is six hundred threescore and six."

Man's failure: Did not repent even though God's wrath was poured out on them.

> (Rev. 9:20-21) "And the rest of the men which were not killed by these plagues yet repented not of the works of their hands, that they should not worship devils, and idols of gold and silver, and brass, and stone, and of wood: which neither can see, nor hear, nor walk: Neither repented they of their murders, nor of their sorceries, nor of their fornication, nor of their thefts."

The Judgment: Israel on earth, The Great Whore, Nations at Armageddon on earth, and the Church in the air at the Judgment Seat of Christ.

> (Jer. 30:7) "Alas! for that day is great, so that none is like it: it is even the time of Jacob's trouble; but he shall be saved out of it."
> (Rev. 17:1) "And there came one of the seven angels which had the seven vials, and talked with me, saying unto me, Come hither; I will shew unto thee the judgment of the great whore that sitteth upon many waters."
> (Rev. 16:16) "And he gathered them together into a place called in the Hebrew tongue Armageddon."
> (Rom. 14:10) "For we shall all stand before the judgment seat of Christ."

Salvation: Faith and works with no new birth or permanent indwelling of the Holy Spirit.

> (Rev. 14:12) "Here is the patience of the saints: here are they that keep the commandments of God, and the faith of Jesus."

Object of God's dealing: The Nation of Israel.

> (Rom. 11:25-26) "For I would not, brethren that ye should be ignorant of this mystery, lest ye should be wise in your own conceits, that blindness in part is happened to Israel, until the fullness of the Gentiles be come in. And so all Israel shall be saved: as it is

written, There shall come out of Sion the Deliverer, and shall turn away ungodliness from Jacob:"

IN THIS DISPENSATION:

1) God again will be dealing with Israel as a nation.
2) The signs will again be in effect.
3) There will be 144,000 sealed, physical, orthodox Jews on this earth preaching.
4) A person called the antichrist will have free reign on this earth.
5) There will be strange phenomenon in the heavens.
6) The sun will get hotter.
7) The mark of the Beast will be in effect.
8) There will be two witnesses who are killed, resurrected, and raptured into heaven.
9) The signs will be in effect since God is dealing with Israel.
10) Other names for this dispensation are Time of Jacob's Trouble and The Great Tribulation.
11) For more on this dispensation see Chapter 12.

8. The Millennial Reign

This Dispensation is called Millennial because it is the Thousand Year Reign of Christ, Millennium means one Thousand.

Length of Dispensation: 1000 years.

(Rev 20:4) "And they lived and reigned with Christ a thousand years."

Beginning: Second Advent of Christ.

(Rev. 19:11) "And I saw heaven opened, and behold a white horse; and he that sat upon him was called Faithful and True, and in righteousness he doth judge and make war."

Ending: Battle of Gog and Magog.

(Rev. 20:8,9) "And shall go out to deceive the nations which are in the four quarters of the earth, Gog and Magog, to gather them together to battle: the number of whom is as the sand of the sea. And they went up on the breadth of the earth, and compassed the camp of the saints about, and the beloved city: and fire came down from God out of heaven, and devoured them."

Man's responsibility: To follow the constitution of the kingdom which is Matthew 5-7 and anything else the King commands.

Man's failure: Gives in to the temptation by Satan to rebel against God.

> (Rev. 20:8,9) Refer to "ending".

The Judgment: God consumes them with fire.

> (Rev. 20:8,9) Refer to "ending".

Salvation: Purely works. There is no need for faith in Jesus because He will be sitting on David's throne in Jerusalem. No new birth or indwelling of the Holy Spirit.

> (Luke 1:32) "He shall be great, and shall be called the Son of the Highest: and the Lord God shall give unto him the throne of his father David."

Object of God's dealing: The whole human race as made up of nations:

> (Rev. 20:8) "And shall go out to deceive the nations which are in the four quarters of the earth."

IN THIS DISPENSATION:

1) People will live again to extraordinary ages.

2) Animals which hunt and animals that are their prey will eat together.
3) Children will play by poisonous snakes.
4) The devil will be bound.
5) There will be painless childbirth.
6) Weather will be perfect.
7) There will be a perfect Judge.
8) People sowing and reaping will overlap.
9) Another name for the Millennial Reign is The Kindom of Heaven.
10) For more on this dispensation see Chapter 11.

9. How Dispensations Relate to Books of the Bible

We will now consider how dispensations relate to the books of the Bible. This is done to show the reader how each book fits dispensationally within the scripture. This information should help the Church Age Christian understand doctrinally where he is, and just as importantly, where he is not.

The first three dispensations which are **Innocence**, **Conscience**, and **Human Government** are found from start to finish in the first eleven chapters of the Book of Genesis. After reading the preceding chapters on the Dispensations it should be abundantly clear that these scriptures do not doctrinally apply to a Christian in the Church Age.

The next dispensation is that of **Promise**. It spans from Genesis Chapter 12 to Exodus Chapter 20. This promise is to Abraham and does not apply to a Church Age Christian.

Following the Dispensation of promise is the Dispensation of **Law**. It began in Exodus Chapter 20 and continues to the crucifixion in the four Gospels with the exception of the Book of Job. (Because Job is the oldest Book of the Bible and is set in the Dispensation of **Promise**). This covers the giving of the Law, the Prophets, the Tribe and lineage of Jesus Christ, His birth, death, burial, and resurrection.

The four Gospels are doctrinally under law. Matthew is one of the transitional books which makes the transition from the Old Testament to the New Testament.

The Gospel of John has the hint of grace in it because of the date of its writing. It was written in 85 to 90 A.D. which was after Paul had completed his writings.

The next Book in order is Acts. It is a transitional book that moves from Israel to the Church. Acts, as the Book of Matthew, is not the place for a Christian to get his doctrine.

Once the transitions from Israel to the Church and the Old Testament to the New Testament take place you are doctrinally in the Church Age. This dispensation was not specifically prophesied in the Old Testament. There are some obscure hints at it through references to night or darkness. Israel had two opportunities to accept Jesus Christ as its Messiah but rejected Him both times. The first rejection culminated in the crucifixion of Christ and the second one resulted in the stoning of Stephen. God then stopped dealing with Israel as a nation. He then began to deal with people on an individual basis. This puts Jew and Gentile alike in a mutual, spiritual body called the Church.

> (1 Cor. 12:13) "For by one Spirit are we all baptized into one body, whether we be Jews or Gentiles, whether we be bond or free; and have been all made to drink into one Spirit."

This placement was contingent on a new birth:

> (John 3:3) "Jesus answered and said unto him, verily, verily, I say unto thee, Except a man be born again, he cannot see the kingdom of God."

The Apostle Paul wrote thirteen Books to the Church. These Books are: Romans, First Corinthians, Second Corinthians, Galatians, Ephesians, Colossians,

Philippians, First Thessalonians, Second Thessalonians, First Timothy, Second Timothy, Titus, and Philemon. You have to take into consideration that Paul was the Apostle to the Gentiles:

> (Rom. 11:13) "For I speak to you Gentiles, inasmuch as I am the apostle of the Gentiles, I magnify mine office."

In these Books you will find the signs are gone except for 1 Corinthians 14 where God allowed them to speak in tongues for a short while early on because of the presence of unbelieving Jews. There is no question that the signs were gone by the time Paul wrote to Timothy. Paul told Timothy to take medicine for a stomach ache:

> (1 Tim. 5:23) "Drink no longer water, but use a little wine for thy stomach's sake and thine often infirmities."

Also he couldn't heal one of his friends:

> (2 Tim. 4:20) "Erastus abode at Corinth: but Trophimus have I left at Miletum sick."

In none of these thirteen books will you find anyone who can lose their salvation. Once you are saved you are saved forever. You cannot lose your salvation no matter what you do. For more on eternal security and signs refer to chapter 10.

The next book on the list is Hebrews. Like Matthew and Acts it is a transitional book. The transition here is from the Church Age to the Great Tribulation.

The Books of the Bible that doctrinally apply to the Great Tribulation are Hebrews, James, First Peter, Second Peter, First John, Second John, Third John, Jude and Revelation. The doctrine contained in these books is what one will need to get through the tribulation.

Lastly the scripture that doctrinally applies to those in the Messianic Dispensation is found in Matthew 5, 6 and 7. You know this by the constant reference to the Kingdom of Heaven in these chapters. These verses inform the individual in the Millennial Reign how they are to conduct themselves and what will happen if they don't conform to these rules.

A further study of doctrine, as it pertains to the Books of the Bible and Bible dispensations will reveal that doctrine from other dispensations can apply to the Church Age Christian. This statement is not based on the opinion of anyone. It is based on scripture:

> (2 Tim. 3:16) "All scripture is given by inspiration of God, and is profitable for doctrine."

If you can, in fact, apply doctrine from other dispensations to a Church Age Christian, how could you do it without violating the doctrine in the thirteen Books Paul wrote to the Church? There is a rule of thumb in these situations, which is: if it doesn't contradict any of the scripture in Paul's writings then you can apply it. If it contradicts you can't apply it. For example:

> (James 2:24) "You see then how that by works a man is justified, and not by faith only."

This verse tells you plainly that works are needed equally as faith to justify the man.

> (Gal. 2:16) "Knowing that a man is not justified by the works of the law, but by faith of Jesus Christ, even we have believed in Jesus Christ, that we might be justified by the faith of Christ, and not by the works of the law: for by the works of the law shall no flesh be justified."

This verse states the complete opposite of James 2:24, therefore it contradicts. To arrive at the correct solution to this problem you have to rightly divide. You do this by placing the Book of James doctrinally in the Tribulation period where God will be dealing with the Jews again. You know this because James 2:24 states that faith and works are both involved in someone's salvation which is how one is saved in the tribulation. Also you have to consider who James is written to:

> (James 1:1) "To the twelve tribes which are scattered abroad, greeting."

The twelve tribes are literal, physical, orthodox Jews:

> (Rev. 7:4-8) "And I heard the number of them which were sealed: and there were sealed and hundred and forty and four thousand of all the tribes of the children of Israel. Of the tribe of Juda were sealed twelve thousand. Of the tribe of Reuben were sealed twelve thousand. Of the tribe of Gad were sealed twelve thousand. Of the tribe of Aser were sealed twelve thousand.

Of the tribe of Nepthalim were sealed twelve thousand. Of the tribe of Manasses were sealed twelve thousand. Of the tribe of Simeon were sealed twelve thousand. Of the tribe of Levi were sealed twelve thousand. Of the tribe of Issachar were sealed twelve thousand. Of the tribe of Zabulon were sealed twelve thousand. Of the tribe of Joseph were sealed twelve thousand. Of the tribe of Benjamin were sealed twelve thousand."

Upon learning this you then place Gal. 2:16 in the Church Age because it is one of the thirteen Books Paul wrote to the Church. You then correctly apply it to a Church Age Christian who only requires faith to be saved. To handle this any other way is to handle God's Word with deceit:

(2 Cor. 4:2) "Nor handling the word of God deceitfully."

Since we have established that the Book of James is doctrinally written to the Jews in the tribulation, let us consider a verse in James that can be doctrinally applied to the Church Age Christian:

(James 3:6) "And the tongue is a fire, a world of iniquity: so is the tongue among our members, that it defileth the whole body, and setteth on fire the course of nature; and it is set on fire of hell."

This verse does not contradict or stand in opposition to any verse in the thirteen books that Paul wrote. In fact it goes along with Paul's doctrine:

> (1 Tim. 5:13) "And withal they learn to be idle, wandering about from house to house; and not only idle, but tattlers also and busy bodies, speaking things which they ought not."

Another example:

> (James 4:7) "Submit yourself therefore to God. Resist the devil, and he will flee from you."

This verse instructs us of what to do to get the devil away from us. This verse also goes along with Paul's doctrine. To prove this, observe this verse in Ephesians:

> (Eph. 6:11) "Put on the whole armour of God, that ye may be able to stand against the wiles of the devil."

There are many other examples of verses from other dispensations that can be doctrinally applied to a Church Age Christian. The previous examples should give the reader an idea of how to Rightly Divide (2 Tim. 2:15).

Concerning the transitional Books of Matthew, Acts, and Hebrews we will give the reader the transitions that take place within these books. The Book of Matthew makes the transition from the Old Testament to the New Testament. The Book of Acts makes the transition from

Israel to the Church. The Book of Hebrews makes the transition from the Church Age to the Great Tribulation.

In these Books you will find people doing and saying things that stand in direct doctrinal opposition to the thirteen books Paul wrote to the Church. The main reason for this is that each of these three books is doctrinally for a time when God is dealing with the Jews. When the Jew is being dealt with it is as a nation not individuals:

> (Rom. 11:26) "And so all Israel shall be saved."

When God deals with the Jews it will always involve signs:

> (1 Cor. 1:22) "For the Jews require a sign."

If the reader will observe, there are changes taking place in these books. The Church Age Christian will do well to be extremely cautious when trying to apply them to themselves.

Every person reading this should take time to acquire some literature from the Charismatics, Church of Christ, Pentecostals, and a number of so-called denominations and find out for yourself what scripture they base their doctrinal stands on. When and if you do this, you will discover a startling pattern. Almost every cult bases its doctrine on verses in Matthew, Acts, and Hebrews. Almost every heresy in the Church Age comes from one or a combination of two or more of these books.

10. Church Age Doctrine

As previously mentioned the doctrine for the Church Age is laid out in the thirteen books written by Paul. These books are Romans through Philemon. There are other books from which you can apply certain scriptures doctrinally to the Church as long as it doesn't contradict anything in the thirteen books. I realize that I have repeated myself but certain things are important enough to repeat. Plus, the best way to learn is repetition.

Since the dispensations and the books they dispensationally fall in have been laid out, rightly dividing can be accomplished. Remember any other avenue will only result in false doctrine.

With this being understood, key doctrinal points for the Church Age can be made without altering the King James Bible. This approach will spark controversy among those who believe and teach false doctrine. However, this approach will not leave the reader with loose ends as trying to apply the whole Bible to every person in every age will.

In this chapter Church Age doctrine will be examined. Doctrines for the Dispensation of Law, The Great Tribulation, and the Millennial Reign will also be examined for the sole purpose of showing the false doctrine presented when scripture isn't rightly divided.

THE BAPTISM OF THE HOLY GHOST

This is one of the most misunderstood points of doctrine. The problem with misunderstanding the Baptism of the Holy Ghost is you actually have to twist the scripture to make a heresy of it. What does the Bible say about the Baptism of the Holy Ghost? There is only one true baptism for the body of Christ:

> (Eph. 4:5) "One Lord, one faith, one baptism."

This one baptism is Spirit baptism. The scripture says the Holy Spirit baptizes us into one body:

> (1 Cor. 12:13) "For by one Spirit are we all baptized into one body, whether we be Jews or Gentiles, whether we be bond or free; and have been all made to drink into one Spirit."

This Body is the Church:

> (Col. 1:18) "And he is the head of the body, the Church; who is the beginning, the firstborn from the dead; that in all things he might have the preeminence."

The baptism occurs at the time of salvation. This baptism not only saves but is the very thing that water baptism is a figure of:

> (1 Pet. 3:21) "The like figure where unto even baptism doth also now save us (not the putting away of the filth of the flesh, but the answer of a good conscience toward God,) by the resurrection of Jesus Christ."

To be saved you have to trust Christ. When you trust Christ, you are baptized with the Holy Spirit:

(Eph. 1:12-13) "That we should be to the praise of his glory, who first trusted in Christ. In whom ye also trusted, after that ye heard the word of truth, the gospel of your salvation: in whom also after that ye believed, ye were sealed with that Holy Spirit of Promise."

When a person is saved and is baptized into Christ's Body, that person is also baptized into His death:

(Rom. 6:3) "Know ye not, that so many of us as were baptized into Jesus Christ were baptized into his death?"

That person trusting Christ is buried with Him in Spirit baptism into His death:

(Rom. 6:5) "For if we have been planted together in the likeness of his death, we shall be also in the likeness of his resurrection."

If we are dead with Jesus Christ unto sin we will also live with Him eternally:

(Rev. 1:18) "I am he that liveth, and was dead; and, behold, I am alive for evermore, Amen: and have the keys of hell and of death."

A Church Age Christian receives the Spirit by the hearing of faith:

> (Gal. 3:2) "This only would I learn of you, Received ye the Spirit by the works of the law, or by the hearing of faith?"

Upon believing in or trusting in Jesus Christ, you receive the baptism of the Holy Ghost. You also receive eternal life:

> (John 3:16) "For God so loved the world, that he gave his only begotten Son, that whosoever believeth in him should not perish, but have everlasting life."

If you don't get the baptism of the Holy Ghost you don't get saved or the indwelling of the Holy Spirit:

> (Rom. 8:9) "But ye are not in the flesh, but in the Spirit, if so be that the Spirit of God dwell in you. Now if any man have not the Spirit of Christ, he is none of his."

The initial evidence of the baptism of the Holy Ghost is the person whom the Holy Ghost indwells becomes a new creature:

> (2 Cor. 5:17) "Therefore if any man be in Christ, he is a new creature: old things are passed away; behold, all things are become new."

Inner conflict begins when a sinner receives Jesus Christ:

(Rom. 7:15) "For that which I do I allow not: for what I would, that do I not: but what I hate, that do I."

The baptism of the Holy Ghost is not something that happens separate from salvation.

The initial evidence of the Holy Ghost is not speaking in tongues. It is a rushing mighty wind:

(Acts 2:2) "And suddenly there came a sound from heaven as of a rushing mighty wind, and it filled all the house where they were sitting."

SALVATION

Salvation in the Church Age is by grace through faith. No one can earn salvation by works or any other way:

(Eph. 2:8,9) "For by grace are ye saved through faith; and that not of yourselves: it is the gift of God: Not of works, lest any man should boast."

To be saved in the Church Age the lost has to trust what Jesus Christ did at Calvary:

(Eph. 1:12,13) "That we should be to the praise of his glory, who first trusted in Christ. In whom ye also trusted, after that ye heard the word of truth, the gospel of your salvation: in whom also after that ye believed, ye were sealed with that Holy Spirit of promise."

You absolutely cannot earn salvation:

(Rom. 4:4,5) "Now to him that worketh is the reward not reckoned of grace, but of debt. But to him that worketh not, but believeth on him that justifieth the ungodly, his faith is counted for righteousness."

Salvation is not according to works:

(2 Tim. 1:9) "Who hath saved us, and called us with an holy calling, not according to our works, but according to his own purpose and grace, which was given us in Christ Jesus before the world began."
(Titus 3:5) "Not by works of righteousness which we have done, but according to his mercy he saved us, by the washing of regeneration, and renewing of the Holy Ghost."

No one is justified by works but by the faith of Jesus Christ:

(Gal. 2:16) "Knowing that a man is not justified by the works of the law, but by the faith of Jesus Christ, even we have believed in Jesus Christ, that we might be justified by the faith of Christ, and not by the works of the law: for by the works of the law shall no flesh be justified."

It has now been established that works has nothing to do with a Church Age Christian's salvation. But works has everything to do with earned rewards at the Judgment Seat of Christ. Works will be judged. The Christian's soul will not be judged. It was judged at his conversion. He was found innocent of any sin. This is because he received Christ's righteousness. It was imputed to him at the time of his conversion:

> (Rom. 4:22,24) "And therefore it was imputed to him for righteousness. Now it was not written for his sake alone, that it was imputed to him; But for us also, to whom it shall be imputed, if we believe on him that raised up Jesus our Lord from the dead."

There are dispensations when works are a part of salvation. The examples used here are under the Dispensation of Law, the Great Tribulation, and the Millennial Reign.

The Ten Commandments were given to start the Dispensation of Law. God gave an additional six hundred plus laws to follow. These can be found in the Books of Exodus, Leviticus, Numbers and Deuteronomy.

> (Exo. 20:1,17) "And God spake all these words, saying... Thou shalt not covet they neighbor's house, thou shalt not covet thy neighbor's wife, nor his manservant, nor his maidservant, nor his ox, nor his ass, nor anything that is thy neighbor's."

In the Great Tribulation a person is saved by faith and works. This is stated so plainly that you only need read a few scriptures to understand this. A person has to endure unto the end:

> (Matt. 24:13) "But he that shall endure unto the end, the same shall be saved."

Faith and works is the means of salvation:

> (Rev. 12:17) "And the dragon was wroth with the woman, and went to make war with the remnant of her seed, which keep the commandments of God, and have the testimony of Jesus Christ."
>
> (Rev. 14:12) "Here is the patience of the saints: here are they that keep the commandments of God, and the faith of Jesus."

In the Millennial Reign salvation is by works only. This is known because Jesus Christ will physically be sitting on the throne of David in Jerusalem. His reign will start here and will last forever:

> (Luke 1:31-33) "And, behold, thou shalt conceive in thy womb, and bring forth a son, and shalt call his name JESUS. He shall be great, and shall be called the Son of the Highest: and the Lord God shall give unto him the throne of his father David: And he shall reign over the house of Jacob forever; and of his kingdom there shall be no end."

Why would anyone need faith in Christ if He is physically sitting on the throne in Jerusalem? Faith is the evidence of things <u>not</u> seen.

No person in the Church Age can work for salvation in any way. Dispensations do exist where works are involved in someone being saved. It just is not in the Dispensation of Grace. This will be explained further under eternal security.

ETERNAL SECURITY

Eternal Security or "once saved always saved" is not just a Baptist doctrine, it is a Bible doctrine. It only applies to Church Age Christians. The reason most Christians don't believe this well documented doctrine is because they either apply doctrine from another age to themselves or they want to have a part in their salvation.

Every Christian should take the time to read Romans through Philemon. Within the confines of these thirteen books nothing will be found written there that even vaguely hints that anyone can lose his salvation. The reason being is no one in the Church can lose his salvation. Make no mistake about it: if you could lose your salvation you would.

Doctrinally and scripturally speaking there is no question that once you are saved you can never be lost again, regardless of what you do. There is nothing that God ever created that can separate born again believers from God thus causing them to lose their salvation.

> (Rom. 8:38,39) "For I am persuaded, that neither death, nor life, nor angels, nor principalities, nor powers, nor things present, nor things to come, nor height, nor depth, nor any other creature, shall be able to separate us from the love of God, which is in Christ Jesus our Lord."

When a person in the Church Age is converted they become a new creature:

> (2Cor. 5:17) "Therefore if any man be in Christ, he is a new creature: old things are passed away; behold, all things are become new."

Those who believe a Church Age Christian can lose his salvation agree that works is the deciding factor. In other words, if your works are good you retain your salvation. If your works are bad, you will lose your salvation. Just as sure as works cannot save anyone in the Church Age, works cannot cause anyone to lose his salvation. Romans 8:38,39 specifically says that no creature can cause someone to lose their salvation. 2 Corinthians 5:17 specifically states when a person is saved they are a new creature. Scripturally speaking, you as a person, your works, or anything else cannot cause you to be lost after you have been saved.

When a person trusts Christ as his Saviour a spiritual operation takes place inside of him. The Holy Spirit cuts the soul and flesh apart. This separates the soul from the sins of the flesh.

> (Col. 2:11,12) "In whom also ye are circumcised with the circumcision made without hands, in putting off the body of the sins of the flesh by the circumcision of Christ: Buried with him in baptism, wherein also ye are risen with him through the faith of the operation of God, who hath raised him from the dead."

Have you ever heard of anyone having a physical circumcision reversed? After the Holy Spirit performs the operation He then seals the soul so it can never again be marred by sin. The soul stays sealed until this fleshly body is redeemed:

> (Eph. 1:13) "In whom ye also trusted, after that ye heard the word of truth, the gospel of your salvation: in whom also after that ye believed, ye were sealed with that Holy Spirit of promise."
> (Eph. 4:30) "And grieve not the Holy Spirit of God, whereby ye are sealed unto the day of redemption."

The problem with Christians who believe they can lose their salvation is simple: They believe that sin has the same effect on their soul as it does on their flesh. In light of Colossians 2:11, 12 this belief is simply untrue. You can have bad works and suffer loss but you (your soul) shall be saved:

> (1Cor. 3:15) "If any man's work shall be burned, he shall suffer loss: but he himself shall be saved; yet so as by fire."

As opposed to your soul your flesh is in a different category altogether. The long range effect sin has on your flesh is death:

> (Gen. 3:3) "But of the fruit of the tree which is in the midst of the garden, God hath said, Ye shall not eat of it, neither shall ye touch it, lest ye die."

The day to day effect that sin has on the flesh is it causes us to go against the will of God. The Apostle Paul was the greatest Christian that ever lived. He said he not only did wrong but he did evil. Do you think Paul was worried that his works would send him to hell? Of course he wasn't:

> (Rom. 7:14-25) "For we know that the law is spiritual: but I am carnal, sold under sin. For that which I do I allow not: for what I would, that do I not; but what I hate, that do I. If then I do that which I would not, I consent unto the law that it is good. Now then it is no more I that do it, but sin that dwelleth in me. For I know that in me (that is, in my flesh,) dwelleth no good thing: for to will is present with me; but how to perform that which is good I find not. For the good that I would I do not, that I do. but the evil which Now if I do that I would not, it is no more I that do it, but sin that dwelleth in me. I find then a law, that, when I would do good, evil is present with me. For I delight in the law of God after the inward man: But I see another law in my members, warring against the law of my mind, and bringing me into captivity to the law of sin which is in my members. O wretched man that I am! Who shall deliver me from the body of this death? I thank God through Jesus Christ our Lord. So then with the mind I myself serve the law of God; but with the flesh, the law of sin."

It has now been established that no where in scripture does it say a Church Age Christian can lose his salvation. What happens then when a Christian sins against Jesus Christ? Don't get the mistaken idea that a person who believes in Eternal Security thinks he can do anything he wants and get by with it. A Church Age Christian, who knows the scripture, knows that when he willfully sins against God and doesn't repent and restore fellowship with God, he receives chastisement. Simply stated, the Lord will punish him in a fashion that is designed to bring him back into fellowship with God. This correction is not only used to bring the Christian back into good spiritual standing with God but yields righteousness unto those who receive it:

> (Heb. 12:5-11) "And ye have forgotten the exhortation which speaketh unto you as unto children, My son, despise not thou the chastening of the Lord, nor faint when thou art rebuked of him: For whom the Lord loveth he chasteneth, and scourgeth every son whom he receiveth. If ye endure chastening God dealeth with you as with sons; for what son is he whom the father chasteneth not? But if ye be without chastisement, whereof all are partakers, then are ye bastards, and not sons. Furthermore we have had fathers of our flesh which corrected us, and we gave them reverence: shall we not much rather be in subjection unto the Father of spirits, and live? For they verily for a few days chastened us after their own pleasure; but he for our profit, that we might be partakers of his holiness. Now no chastening for the present seemeth to be joyous, but grievous: nevertheless afterward it yieldeth the peaceable fruit of

righteousness unto them which are exercised thereby."

There are times when a Christian is chastened but still doesn't repent. This results in physical death:

> (Rom. 8:13) "For if ye live after the flesh, ye shall die: but if ye through the Spirit do mortify the deeds of the body, ye shall live."

There is an example of a Christian, in the Bible, that conclusively proves he will lose his mortal life if he doesn't respond to chastisement or rebuking. This scripture names the sin, and condemns the Church of Corinth for allowing it to go on. In addition this scripture states that a certain man is sinning willfully, will not stop his sinful way (repent), and Satan will be allowed by God to physically kill this man. Upon death this man will go to be with Christ to await the Rapture of the Church. Because that man is saved:

> (1 Cor. 5:1-5) "It is reported commonly that there is fornication among you, and such fornication as is not so much as named among the Gentiles, that one should have his father's wife.... that he that hath done this deed might be taken away from among you. For I verily, as absent in body, but present in spirit, have judged already, as though I were present, concerning him that hath so done this deed. In the name of our Lord Jesus Christ, when ye are gathered together, and my spirit, with the power of our Lord Jesus Christ. To deliver such an one unto Satan for the destruction of the flesh, that the spirit may be saved in the day of the Lord Jesus."

When a person accepts Christ as his Saviour, Jesus knows that person:

> (John 10:27) "My sheep hear my voice, and I know them, and they follow me."

If a person can be lost after they had been saved, how could Jesus Christ say He never knew him. Jesus didn't say that He knew the person at one time but not now. He said He never knew him:

> (Mat.. 7:19,23) "Every tree that bringeth not forth good fruit is hewn down, and cast into the fire."
> And then will I profess unto them, I never knew you: depart from me, ye that work iniquity."

If a saved person is known of God (which he is) and then Christ told this same person at any time, after saving that person, He never knew him, wouldn't he be lying?

> (Heb. 6:18) "That by two immutable things, in which it was impossible for God to lie."

If it were possible (and it isn't) for a Christian to be saved then lost, that person would have to remain lost forever. This business of a person being saved, lost, then, saved again is not only utter nonsense, it is rejection of the Word of God. The Bible says it is impossible for a person to be saved, lost, then saved again.

> (Heb. 6:4-6) "For it is impossible for those who were once enlightened, and have tasted

of the heavenly gift, and were made partakers of the Holy Ghost, and have tasted the good word of God, and the powers of the world to come, if they shall fall away, to renew them again unto repentance; seeing they crucify to themselves the Son of God afresh, and put him to an open shame."

Why then do some Church Age Christians believe they can be lost after they are saved? These Christians are reading about someone in scripture who can lose his salvation. The problem begins when they apply this doctrinally to themselves. This is tribulation doctrine and cannot be applied to a Christian. For example: To "endure unto the end" is something written to those in the Tribulation Period or until he gets his head cut off because he rejects the mark of the beast. The abomination of desolation takes place during Daniel's Seventieth Week or the Tribulation Period:

> (Matt. 24:13-15) "But he that shall endure unto the end, the same shall be saved. And this gospel of the kingdom shall be preached in all the world for a witness unto all nations; and then shall the end come. When ye therefore shall see the abomination of desolation, spoken of by Daniel the prophet, stand in the holy place, (whoso readeth, let him understand.)"
> (Mark 13:13,14) "And ye shall be hated of all men for my names sake: but he that shall endure unto the end, the same shall be saved. But when ye shall see the abomination of desolation, spoken of by

> Daniel the prophet, standing where it ought not, (let him that readeth understand.)"

What if someone sins willfully after he is saved? There remains no more sacrifice for sin. What is left is fearfully looking for judgment and indignation connected with fire. Where do these verses fit dispensationally? In light of 1 Corinthians 5:1-5, and knowing that the Book of Hebrews is a transitional book that is aimed doctrinally at the Great Tribulation. Therefore it has to be tribulation doctrine:

> (Heb. 10:26,27) "For if we sin willfully after that we have received the knowledge of the truth, there remaineth no more sacrifice for sins, but a certain fearful looking for of judgment and fiery indignation, which shall devour the adversaries."

Summary: During the Church Age no one can earn his salvation by works. No one can keep his salvation by works. To say you can earn or keep your salvation by works is claiming your righteousness equals that of Jesus Christ. Would anyone reading this care to accept the challenge of comparing your righteousness to that of Jesus Christ? I didn't think so. Let us end this thought with scripture:

> (Gen. 6:5) "And God saw that the wickedness of man was great in the earth, and that every imagination of the thoughts of his heart was only evil continually."
> (Isa. 64:6) "But we are all as an unclean thing, and all our righteousness are as filthy rags; and we all do fade as a leaf; and our

iniquities, like the wind, have taken us away."

(Rom. 3:24-26) "Being justified freely by his grace through the redemption that is in Jesus Christ: Whom God hath set forth to be propitiation through faith in his blood to declare his righteousness for the remission of sins that are past, through the forbearance of God; To declare, I say, at this time his righteousness: that he might be just, and the justifier of him which believeth in Jesus."

SIGNS

The subject of signs seems to be always in the forefront of controversy. This includes tongues, healing, handling snakes etc... Before a person can intelligently discuss signs, that person has to have a Biblical perspective of what signs are and are not. Any time a sign is mentioned in scripture it is connected to the Jews. Apart from the Jew there are no signs, remember that. As you will find this isn't anyone's opinion it is clear Biblical truth. Let us now examine what the scripture says about signs.

Signs originated with the nation of Israel. The first man to ever get sick was Moses. He had leprosy. Moses was also the first man to get healed. Healing is a sign. The nation of Israel began with a sign.

(Exo. 4:6-8) "And the Lord said furthermore unto him, put now thine hand into thy bosom, and he put his hand into his bosom: and when he took it out, behold, his hand was leprous as snow. And he said, put thine hand into thy bosom again. And he put his

> hand into his bosom again; and plucked it out of his bosom, and, behold, it was turned again as his other flesh. And it shall come pass, if they will not believe thee, neither hearken to the voice of the first sign, that they will believe the voice of the latter sign."

Was Moses a Jew? Yes, Moses was born a Jew and his brethren were Hebrews:

> (Exo. 2:11) "And it came to pass in those days, when Moses was grown, that he went out unto his brethren, and looked on their burdens: and he spied an Egyptian smiting an Hebrew, one of his brethren."

Since the Nation of Israel began with a sign, they require a sign. The Greek or Gentile does not require a sign, he seeks after wisdom:

> (1 Cor. 1:22) "For the Jews require a sign, and the Greeks seek after wisdom."

Other signs given to Jewish Apostles were casting out devils, speaking in tongues, snake handling, drinking poison, and healing by the laying on of hands. This was voiced by the most authoritative man who ever walked on this earth, Jesus Christ:

> (Mark 16:14-18) "Afterward he appeared unto the eleven as they sat at meat, and upbraided them with their unbelief and hardness of heart, because they believed not them which had seen him after he was risen. And he said unto them, go ye into all the

> world, and preach the gospel to every creature. He that believeth and is baptized shall be saved; but he that believeth not shall be damned. And these signs shall follow them that believe; In my name shall they cast out devils; they shall speak with new tongues; They shall take up serpents; and if they drink any deadly thing, it shall not hurt them; they shall lay hands on the sick, and they shall recover."

Make no mistake about it. If you are seeking after a sign or if your church or pastor is teaching you to speak in tongues or to try to heal people who have sickness, physical deformities, blindness etc... you are not doing God's will you are wicked and adulterous. If you get a sign it is a false sign or one given by Satan because Jesus Christ said He wouldn't give you a sign except His death, burial, and resurrection:

> (Matt. 12:39,40) "But he answered and said unto them, An evil and adulterous generation seeketh after a sign; and there shall no sign be given to it, but the sign of the prophet Jonas: For as Jonas was three days and three nights in the whale's belly; so shall the Son of man be three days and three nights in the heart of the earth."

A Church Age Christian is not to look for a sign. They are to live by faith because this is what a just person does. If you choose to be wicked and adulterous then speak in tongues, try to heal people or attempt to do any number of other signs. It is your choice:

> (Rom. 1:17) "For therein is the righteousness of God revealed from faith to faith: as it is written, the just shall live by faith."

This healing and tongues movement started in the early 1900's and exploded into what it is today (it is usually just healing and tongues, when was the last time you saw one of these "preachers" on television drinking poison or handling snakes?). These dishonest people appear on television and beg for money. They tell you to release your faith by giving them your money. Why aren't these people preaching and healing on the streets and from church to church like Jesus Christ did? (I realize Christ was in the synagogues not churches). If these people could actually do what they claimed they wouldn't have to ask for a dime. People would give them more money than they could possibly spend. Why do they not do this? It is simple: they are liars. How do you know if one of these con men is lying? You try them. How do you try them? You try them by challenging them to do what they say they can do. They will make some stupid, unscriptural excuse and leave. These signs, they claim to have, were given to the apostles. And yes we are to try the false apostles:

> (2 Cor. 12:12) "Truly the signs of an apostle were wrought among you in all patience, in signs, and wonders, and mighty deeds."
> (Rev. 2:2) "I know thy works, and thy labour, and thy patience, and how thou canst not bear them which are evil: and thou hast tried them which say they are apostles, and are not, and hast found them liars."

When some are tried and are found liars they then use the excuse that a person can't get healed because the one being "healed" doesn't have enough faith. According to Jesus Christ you don't have to have faith to be healed. He healed people then marveled because they still had no faith:

> (Mark 6:5,6) "And he could there do no mighty work, save that he laid his hands upon a few sick folk, and healed them. And he marveled because of their unbelief."

The truth of the matter is the one who prays for the sick is the one whose faith comes into play:

> (James 5:15) "And the prayer of faith shall save the sick, and the Lord shall raise him up."

Something else you will hear from these "healers" is that no one is meant to be sick. All people are supposed to be well. Some people were sick because God is to be made manifest through their healing. They were meant to be sick:

> (John 9:1-3) "And as Jesus passed by, he saw a man which was blind from his birth. And his disciples asked him, saying, Master, who did sin, this man, or his parents, that he was born blind? Jesus answered, neither hath this man sinned, nor his parents: but that the works of God should be made manifest in him."

The Apostle Paul, one of the greatest healers that ever lived, had an infirmity all the time he was in the ministry:

(2 Cor. 12:7-9) "And lest I should be exalted above measure through the abundance of the revelations, there was given to me a thorn in the flesh, the messenger of Satan to buffet me, lest I should be exalted above measure. For this thing I besought the Lord thrice, that it might depart from me. And he said unto me, my grace is sufficient for thee: for my strength is made perfect in weakness. Most gladly therefore will I rather glory in my infirmities, that the power of Christ may rest upon me."

Tongues is another subject that draws a lot of attention. People say tongues are a number of things. The Bible settles all the controversy. Tongues are a sign for unbelieving Jews:

(1 Cor. 14:22) "Wherefore tongues are for a sign, not to them that believe, but to them that believe not."

Some claim tongues are a prayer language. These people attempt to prove this by using a verse of scripture that has nothing to do with praying in tongues. This verse states "if" someone prayed in tongues his spirit prays. It isn't telling anyone to do it. It is stating if someone did pray in tongues his understanding would be unfruitful. If you are going to rightfully divide you have to realize praying in tongues is a bad thing, it is unfruitful. Because the unlearned will not understand what you are saying. You cannot edify the ignorant with tongues:

> (1 Cor. 14:14) "For if I pray in an unknown tongue, my spirit prayeth, but my understanding is unfruitful."
>
> (1 Cor. 14:16,17) "Else when thou shalt bless with the spirit, how shall he that occupieth the room of the unlearned say Amen at thy giving of thanks, seeing he understandeth not what thou sayest? For thou verily givest thanks well, but the other is not edified."

There are those who believe that the initial evidence of the Holy Ghost is speaking in tongues. This perversion is arrived at by transferring the unknown tongues from 1 Corinthians 14 to Acts 2, which they are not. Every tongue in Acts 2 is a known language. Then trying to fit the Baptism of the Holy Ghost unto 1 Corinthians 14. There is not even a hint of the Baptism of the Holy Ghost in 1 Corinthians 14. Read it and see for yourself. Notice again when someone speaks in tongues, Jews are present (Acts 5:5).

> (Acts 2:1-6) "And when the day of Pentecost was fully come they were all with one accord in one place. And suddenly there came a sound from heaven as of a rushing mighty wind, and it filled all the house where they were sitting. And there appeared unto them cloven tongues like as of fire, and it sat upon each of them. And they were all filled with the Holy Ghost, and began to speak with other tongues, as the Spirit gave them utterance. And there were dwelling at Jerusalem Jews, devout men, out of every nation under heaven. Now when this was

noised abroad, the multitude came together, and were confounded because that every man heard them speak in his own language."

There are three accounts of tongues in the Bible. Every time tongues were spoken, Jews were present. This is very significant if you want to rightly divide the Word. The Apostles were there speaking tongues in the presence of other Jews. Tongues are for a sign (1 Cor. 14:22) and the Jews seek a sign (1 Cor. 1:22):

> (Acts 2:4) "And they were all filled with the Holy Ghost, and began to speak with other tongues, as the Spirit gave them utterance."
> (Acts 10:45,46) "And they of the circumcision which believed were astonished, as many as came with Peter, because that on the Gentiles also was poured out the gift of the Holy Ghost. For they heard them speak with tongues, and magnify God. Then answered Peter."
> (Acts 19:6) "And when Paul had laid his hands upon them, the Holy Ghost came on them; and they spake with tongues, and prophesied."

Did it ever strike you as being odd that Jesus Christ never spoke in tongues. He never did.

The Bible gives guidelines for speaking in tongues. These guidelines are given in 1 Corinthians 14. In any assembly there is not to be anymore than three involved in speaking in tongues. They are to speak by course or one at a time. One is supposed to interpret:

> (1 Cor. 14:27) "If any man speak in an unknown tongue, let it be by two, or at the most by three, and that by course; and let one interpret."

If there is no interpreter no one is to speak in tongues. They are to keep quiet:

> (1 Cor. 14:28) "But if there be no interpreter, let him keep silence in the church; and let him speak to himself, and to God."

Understanding the fact that tongues are absolutely not for a Church Age Christian let us examine procedure for speaking in tongues in the local Pentecostal, Charismatic, or Apostolic Churches. Have you ever heard or have been told of a woman speaking in tongues? Any woman speaking in tongues is doing it contrary to scripture. Therefore she is being led by Satan. Have you ever heard or have been told about more than three men talking in tongues at one time? If so these men were doing this contrary to scripture. Therefore they were being led by Satan. Have you ever heard or have someone tell you about people speaking in tongues with no interpreter. If so they were doing it contrary to scripture. Therefore they were being led by Satan. Again, tongues are for a sign for unbelieving Jews, not a Church Age Christian.

With the death of the Apostles went the signs. The signs had already stopped by the time Paul was writing to Timothy. Paul told Timothy to take medicine if his stomach hurt:

> (1 Tim. 5:23) "Drink no longer water, but use a little wine for thy stomach's sake and thine of ten infirmities."

Paul couldn't heal his friend Trophimus:

> (2 Tim. 4:20) "Erastus abode at Corinith: but Trophimus have I left at Miletum sick."

These signs stopped because God stopped dealing with the Nation of Israel:

> (Rom. 11:25) "For I would not, brethren, that ye should be ignorant of this mystery, lest ye should be wise in your own conceits, that blindness in part is happened to Israel, until the fullness of the Gentiles become in."

God will deal with Israel again during the Great Tribulation:

> (Dan. 9:27) "And he shall confirm the covenant with many for one week: and in the midst of the week he shall cause the sacrifice and the oblation to lease, and for the overspreading of abominations he shall make it desolate, even until the consummation, and that determined shall be poured upon the desolate."

During this seven year period the signs will return:

> (Rev. 11:6) "These have power to shut heaven, that it rain not in the days of their prophecy: and have power over waters to

turn them to blood, and to smite the earth with all plagues, as often as they will."

What of these false apostles of today? What exactly are they doing? They are trying to attract attention to themselves. They are actually heralding the coming of the man of sin or the antichrist. The antichrist has all power, signs, and wonders but he performs these in deceit:

> (2 Thes. 2:9) "Even him, whose coming is after the working of Satan with all power and signs and lying wonders."

Only when God is dealing with the Jew are the signs in effect. In the Church Age there is no difference between the Jew and Gentile. Therefore the signs are not in effect:

> (Rom. 10:12) "For there is no difference between the Jew and the Greek: for the same Lord over all is rich unto all that call upon his name."

THE RAPTURE

One day, in the future, the Church will leave this earth to meet Jesus Christ in the air. This includes those who are alive at this time and those who are dead in Christ. Those who sleep in death will rise first. Then those who are alive and remain will come afterward. The Christian will hear a loud noise that signals to him that it is time to leave this present evil world. This will begin our eternal, perfect, fellowship with Jesus Christ:

> (1 Thes. 4:14-17) "For if we believe that Jesus died and rose again, even so them also which sleep in Jesus will God bring with him. For this we say unto you by the word of the Lord, that we which are alive and remain unto the coming of the Lord shall not prevent them which are asleep. For the Lord himself shall descend from heaven with a shout, with the voice of the archangel, and with the trump of God: and the dead in Christ shall rise first: Then we which are alive and remain shall be caught up together with them in the clouds to meet the Lord in the air: and so shall we ever be with the Lord."

This rapture or calling out of the Church will be unexplainable.

> (1 Cor. 15:51) "Behold, I shew you a mystery; we shall not all sleep, but we shall all be changed."

It will happen quickly. There will be a loud noise to signal our departure.

> (1 Cor. 15:52) "In a moment, in the twinkling of an eye, at the last trump: for the trumpet shall sound, and the dead shall be raised incorruptible, and we shall be changed."

Your mortal body, subject to corruption or the rotting of the flesh, will be changed. It will be replaced by an eternal body:

> (1 Cor. 15:53) "For this corruptible must put on incorruption, and this mortal must put on immortality."

God will give the Church Age Christian a supernatural body like the one he had on the Mount of Transfiguration:

> (Phil. 3:21) "Who shall change our vile body, that it may be fashioned like unto his glorious body, according to the working whereby he is able even to subdue all things unto himself."
> (Matt. 17:2) "And was transfigured before them: and his face did shine as the sun and his raiment was white as the light."

This supernatural or glorified body is not subject to the laws of nature. It can appear and disappear at will:

> (Luke 24:36) "And as they thus spake, Jesus himself stood in the midst of them, and saith unto them, Peace be unto you."

Death will not have any effect on those alive and the grave cannot hold those that are dead:

> (1 Cor. 15:54-55) "So when this corruptible shall have put on incorruption and this mortal shall have put on immortality, then shall be brought to pass the saying that is

written, death is swallowed up in victory. O death, where is thy sting? O grave, where is thy victory?

In the Book of Revelation you find one of the greatest types of the Church in the Bible. This type is the Apostle John. He saw a door opened in heaven and heard a voice like a trumpet which was calling him out. It said "Come up hither." John then went in the Spirit into the future to see what would take place:

> (Rev. 4:1) "After this I looked, and, behold, a door was opened in heaven: and the first voice which I heard was as it were of a trumpet talking with me; which said, Come up hither, and I will shew thee things which must be hereafter."

In the Book of Revelation the Church is talked about in the first three chapters. The last mention of the churches is in Revelation chapter three:

> (Rev. 3:22) "He that hath an ear, let him hear what the Spirit saith unto the churches."

The Church is not mentioned again until Revelation chapter nineteen. She has been changed from a spiritual army to a physical army:

> (Rev. 19:14) "And the armies which were in heaven followed him upon white horses, clothed in fine linen, white and clean."

We are to wait for Jesus Christ which delivered us, through salvation, from His wrath during the Great

Tribulation. Notice the verse says "delivered" which is past tense. "Wrath to come" is future tense. Because we were saved before the rapture we will not have to go through the Tribulation Period:

> (1 Thes. 1:10) "And to wait for his Son from heaven, whom he raised from the dead, even Jesus, which delivered us from the wrath to come."

We aren't going to obtain or receive Gods wrath because we did what He told us to do. No where in God's Word is anyone punished for doing what God instructed him to do. A good example of this would be to give one of your children specific instruction in how you want him to behave. He follows your instructions to the letter. Then you punish him. Does this make sense to you? This would bring nothing but confusion does God cause confusion?

> (1 Thes. 5:9) "For God hath not appointed us to wrath, but to obtain salvation by our Lord Jesus Christ."
> (1 Cor. 14:33) "For God is not the author of confusion, but of peace, as in all churches of the saints."

The people in the Body of Christ were put in this position by trusting Jesus Christ:

> (1 Cor. 12:13) "For by one Spirit are we baptized into one body, whether we be Jews or Gentiles, whether we be bond or free; and have been all made to drink into one Spirit."

Knowing that Christ will take us off this earth before pouring out His wrath upon those left is to comfort us:

> (1 Thes. 4:18) "Wherefore comfort one another with these words."

The true Church or Body of Christ consists only of those who put their trust in Jesus Christ and have been born again. Before the Great Tribulation Jesus Christ will come and get the true Church. The Church will not go through the Tribulation in whole or in part. Those who think they will go through parts or all of the tribulation want to work their way to heaven. Jesus' blood isn't enough for them evidently.

THE JUDGMENT SEAT OF CHRIST

The Judgment Seat of Christ is the judgment for those in the Church or Body of Christ only. There will be no danger of anyone going to hell at this judgment. It is the place where believers will have their works judged. Only those works done after salvation will be judged:

> (1 Tim. 4:10) "For therefore we both labour and suffer reproach, because we trust in the living God, who is Saviour of all men, specially of those that believe."
> (John 1:29) "The next day John seeth Jesus coming unto him, and saith, Behold the Lamb of God, which taketh away the sin of the world."

The believer himself is not judged because that judgment took place when he trusted Christ. He is made the righteousness of Jesus Christ:

> (2 Cor. 5:21) "For he hath made him to be sin for us, who knew no sin; that we might be made the righteousness of God in him."

Because the believer took on Jesus Christ's righteousness at salvation:

> (Rom. 4:24) "But for us also, to whom it shall be imputed, if we believe on him that raised up Jesus our Lord from the dead."

The Judgment Seat of Christ will take place in the air where the dead and living in Christ will meet:

> (1 Thes. 4:17) "Then we which are alive and remain shall be caught up together with them in the clouds, to meet the Lord in the air: and so shall we ever be with the Lord."

This judgment will reveal what types of work the Christian performed. If it be of high quality as things done because you love God and want to be obedient to Him. These works will go through the fire as gold, silver, and precious stones which will serve to make them more pure. The bad works that were done to satisfy the flesh or win praise of men will go through the fire as wood, hay and stubble which will burn up. If the works survive (good works) the believer will receive a reward. If the works are consumed (bad works) the believer will suffer loss:

(1 Cor. 3:12-15) "Now if any man build upon this foundation gold, silver, precious stones, wood, hay, stubble; Every man's work shall be made manifest: for the day shall declare it, because it shall be revealed by fire; and the fire shall try every man's work of what sort it is. If any man's work abide which he hath built thereupon, he shall receive a reward. If any man's work shall be burned, he shallsuffer loss: but he himself shall be saved; yet so as by fire."

This judging fire will come from the eyes of the glorified King:

(Rev. 1:14) "His head and his hairs were white like wool, as white as snow; and his eyes were as a flame of fire."

Again all Christians will stand before the Judgment Seat of Christ:

(Rom. 14:10) "But why dost thou judge thy brother? Or why dost thou set at nought thy brother? For we shall all stand before the judgment seat of Christ."
(2 Cor. 5:10) "For we must all appear before the judgment seat of Christ: that every one may receive the things done in his body, according to that he hath done, whether it be good or bad."

The rewards given at this judgment will come in the form of crowns. They are five in number and are specifically named in scripture. These crowns are:

1) The Crown of Righteousness is given to those Christians who truly want Jesus Christ to return:

> (2 Tim. 4:8) "Henceforth there is laid up for me a crown of righteousness, which the Lord, the righteous judge, shall give me at that day: and not to me only, but unto all them also that love his appearing."

2) The Crown of Life is given to those who resist temptation. This same crown is given to a martyr. If a person resists temptation he will receive the same reward as a martyr:

> (James 1:12) "Blessed is the man that endureth temptation: for when he is tried, he shall receive the crown of life, which the Lord hath promised to them that love him."
> (Rev. 2:10) "Fear none of those things which thou shalt suffer: behold, the devil shall cast some of you into prison, that ye may be tried; and ye shall have tribulation ten days: be thou faithful unto death, and I will give thee a crown of life."

3) The Incorruptible Crown is given to those who keep their bodies in good physical condition:

> (1 Cor. 9:24-27) "Know ye not that they which run in a race run all, but one receiveth the prize? So run, that ye may obtain. And every man striveth for the mastery is temperate in all things. Now they do it to obtain a corruptible crown; but we an

incorruptible. I therefore so run, no as uncertainly; so fight I, not as one that beateth the air: But I keep under my body, and bring it into subjection: lest that by any means, when I have preached to others, I myself should be a castaway."

4) The Crown of Glory is given to those who feed the flock of God. It can be won by a pastor, missionary, or teacher who spiritually feeds the flock the Word of God:

(1 Pet. 5:1-4) "The elders which are among you I exhort, who am also an elder, and a witness of the sufferings of Christ, and also a partaker of the glory that shall be revealed: Feed the flock of God which is among you, taking the oversight thereof, not by constraint, but willingly; not for filthy lucre, but of a ready mind; Neither as being lords over Gods heritage, but being examples to the flock. And when the chief Shepherd shall appear, ye shall receive a crown of glory that fadeth not away."

5) The Crown of Rejoicing is given to a soul winner:

(1 Thes. 2:19,20) "For what is our hope, or joy, or crown of rejoicing? Are not even ye in the presence of our Lord Jesus Christ at his coming? For ye are our glory and joy."

It is called the Crown of Rejoicing because there is rejoicing in heaven when a soul is saved:

(Luke 15:7) "I say unto you, that likewise joy shall be in heaven over one sinner that repenteth, more than over ninety and nine just persons, which need no repentance."

The Judgment Seat of Christ also supports eternal security. Even if a man's works are bad and are burned he himself shall be saved.

(1 Cor. 3:15) "If any man's work shall be burned, he shall suffer loss: but he himself shall be saved; yet so as by fire."

A Church Age Christian on this earth is not "getting by" with sin. Everything a person does after salvation is works and all his works will be judged. You have a personal relationship with a personal Saviour because you received Him personally. When you reach this judgment you will give a personal account of your works to Jesus Christ because it will be just you and Him: it will be personal.

THE SEVEN MYSTERIES

There are seven mysteries in the Word of God. These mysteries are to be believed and taught. Notice I didn't say understood, I said believed. If the Church would have been faithful and taught these mysteries it probably wouldn't be in such bad shape today. All Christians are to be stewards of these mysteries. The stewards are to be faithful to believe and teach these mysteries.

(1 Cor. 4:1,2) "Let man so account of us, as of the ministers of Christ, and stewards of

the mysteries of God. Moreover it is required in stewards, that a man be found faithful."

These seven mysteries are:

1)   The mystery of Godliness. This mystery is that God came to this earth as a baby through the virgin birth:

> (1 Tim. 3:16) "And without controversy great is the mystery of godliness: God was manifest in the flesh, justified in the Spirit, seen of angels, preached unto the Gentiles, believed on in the world, received up into glory."

2)   The mystery of Christ in you, the hope of glory. This mystery is Jesus Christ taking up residence inside the believer at salvation. This is what will get the believer off the ground at the rapture:

> (1 Col. 1:27) "To whom God would make known what is the riches of the glory of this mystery among the Gentiles; which is Christ in you, the hope of glory."

3)   This mystery concerns Jesus Christ and His bride. When a man or woman gets saved they are spiritually joined to Jesus Christ. We become spiritually one with Jesus similar to a man and a woman who marry become one flesh physically:

> (Eph. 5:25-32) "Husbands, love your wives, even as Christ also loved the church, and gave himself for it; That he might sanctify

> and cleanse it with the washing of water by the word, that he might present it to himself a glorious church, not having spot, or wrinkle, or any such thing; but that it should be holy and without blemish. So ought men to love their wives as their own bodies. He that loveth his wife loveth himself. For no man ever yet hateth his own flesh; but nourisheth and cherisheth it, even as the Lord the church: for we are members of his body, of his flesh, and of his bones. For this cause shall a man leave his father and mother, and shall be joined unto his wife, and they two shall be one flesh. This is a great mystery: but I speak concerning Christ and the church."

4) This mystery tells you that God is not finished with Israel. The rejection of Jesus Christ has brought them some two thousand years of dispersion and grief. They also have the Great Tribulation ahead of them. But God will pour out His wrath on them as a nation during the Tribulation Period. Therefore He will again deal with Israel as a nation and save them:

> (Rom. 11:25,26) "For I would not, brethren, that ye should be ignorant of this mystery, lest ye should be wise in your own conceits, that blindness in part is happened to Israel, until the fullness of the Gentiles be come in. And so all Israel shall be saved: as it is written, There shall come out of Sion the Deliverer, and shall turn away ungodliness from Jacob."

5) The mystery Babylon is next:

> (Rev. 17:5) "And upon her forehead was a name written, MYSTERY, BABYLON THE GREAT, THE MOTHER OF HARLOTS AND ABOMINATIONS OF THE EARTH."

This monstrosity is called a great whore who will be judged by God:

> (Rev. 17:1) "And there came one of the seven angels which had the seven vials. And talked with me, saying unto me, Come hither; I will shew unto thee the judgment of the great whore that sitteth upon many waters."

This great whore is also called a woman who sold herself to the kings of the earth. This act affected the people who lived on earth. She is also connected to the antichrist or the beast:

> (Rev. 17:2,3) "With whom the kings of the earth have committed fornication, and the inhabitants of the earth have been made drunk with the wine of her fornication. So he carried me away in the spirit into the wilderness: and I saw a woman sit upon a scarlet coloured beast, full of names of blasphemy, having seven heads and ten horns."

This woman was dressed in expensive clothing, and decorated with gold, precious stones, and pearls. She also held a golden cup which was full of abominations filthiness which came from her involvement with the world:

> (Rev. 17:4) "And the woman was arrayed in purple and scarlet colour, and decked with gold and precious stones and pearls, having a golden cup in her hand full of abominations and filthiness of her fornication."

This woman killed saints and martyrs. She was so large, powerful, and influential that John wondered with great admiration:

> (Rev. 17:6) "And I saw the woman drunken with the blood of the saints, and with the blood of the martyrs of Jesus: and when I saw her, I wondered with great admiration."

This woman is a city that sits on seven mountains:

> (Rev. 17:9) "And here is the mind which hath wisdom. The seven heads are seven mountains, on which the woman sitteth."
> (Rev. 17:18) "And the woman which thou sawest is that great city, which reigneth over the kings of the earth."

If one puts all this together you get the type of truth that causes division. If you would allow this truth to separate you from what this scripture is referring to, you would be doing God's will.

What city is built on seven mountains? What city houses a religion that killed Christians who didn't conform to its rules? What religion mixes and fits in with the rich and elite of the world? What religion hosts ambassadors from countries? What religion dresses its' leaders in gold, jewels, and very expensive colorful clothing?

The facts of the matter are these: Rome is built on seven mountains. Reference the "R" encyclopedia. Rome the city shares its name with the Roman Catholic religion. Roman Catholics mix and fit in with the rich and elite of the world. The Roman Catholic Church has several business holdings which are mostly tax free. Two of these holdings are a major Brewing Company and Yankee Stadium. The Roman Catholic Church dresses its' leaders in gold, jewelry, and expensive and colorful clothing. Did you see the funeral of Pope John Paul? The Roman Catholics persecuted and killed Christians when they didn't conform to their traditions. Read Foxe's Book of Martyrs.

The reason the Bible calls it a mystery is because Rome is still ruling but in a mystery form. This form is religious. The antichrist can therefore take over the Catholic Church. He will bring about peace and world order and the whole world will follow him. This will result in an absolute monarchy with Satan, as the antichrist, being the monarch or pope.

6) The mystery of iniquity is next. It is the mystery of Satan coming to this earth and literally taking over a human body. He is called the man of sin and son of perdition. He will be against everything that God is for. This mystery of iniquity is going on right now in the form of sin in quantity and openness. People are not ashamed of sin and perversion anymore and the Church will resemble the world so much you won't be able to tell one from the other. Even some churches will welcome the antichrist by trying to steal and imitate the signs given to Isarel.

(2 Thes. 2:2-9) "That ye be not soon shaken in mind, or be troubled, neither by spirit, nor by word, nor by letter as from us, as that the day of Christ is at hand. Let no man deceive you by any means: for that day shall not come, except there come a falling away first, and that man of sin be revealed, the son of perdition; Who opposeth and exalteth himself above all that is called God, or that is worshipped; so that he as God sitteth in the temple of God, shewing himself that he is God. Remember ye not, that, when I was yet with you, I told you these things? And now ye know what withholdeth that he might be revealed in his time. For the mystery of iniquity doth already work: only he who now letteth will let, until he be taken out of the way. And then shall that Wicked be revealed, whom the Lord shall consume with the spirit of his mouth, and shall destroy with the brightness of his coming: Even him, whose coming is after the working of Satan, with all power, and signs, and lying wonders..."

The last mystery is that of the rapture which was covered in some detail previously in this chapter. This is the Church leaving this earth before the Lord pours out His wrath on the Jews and the unsaved who are left behind:

(1 Cor. 15:51-55) "Behold I shew you a mystery; We shall not all sleep, but we shall all be changed, In a moment, in the twinkling of an eye, at the last trump: for the trumpet shall sound, and the dead shall be

raised incorruptible, and we shall be changed. For this corruptible must put on incorruption. So when this corruptible shall have put on incorruption, and this mortal shall have put on immortality, then shall be brought to pass the saying that is written, Death is swallowed up in victory. O death, where is thy sting? O grave, where is thy victory?"

PRIESTS

Let us now examine what the Bible says about priests in the Church Age. Everyone knows that God used priests in the Old Testament. This continued into the gospels. This practice stopped before the New Testament began. When Jesus died on the cross the veil of the temple was rent or ripped. It was rent from top to bottom. This signified we can now come directly to God without needing a priest to intercede for us:

> (Matt. 27:51) "And behold, the veil of the temple was rent in twain from the top to the bottom; and the earth did quake, and the rocks rent."

We can now pray directly to God:

> (Heb. 4:16) "Let us therefore come boldly unto the throne of grace, that we may obtain mercy, and find grace to help in time of need."

We are to call no man on earth our father. This is referring to a religious leader. We are to view no one on earth as being in the place of God:

> (Matt. 23:9) "And call no man your father upon the earth: for one is your Father, which is in heaven."

We are to confess our faults to each other. Not our sins:

> (James 5:16) "Confess your faults one to another, and pray one for another, that ye may be healed. The effectual fervent prayer of a righteous man availeth much."

Men are not to worship men:

> (Acts 14:11-18) "And when the people saw what Paul had done, they lifted up their voices, saying in the speech of Lycaonia, The gods are come down to us in the likeness of men. And they called Barnabas, Jupiter, and Paul, Mercurius, because he was the chief speaker. Then the priest of Jupiter, which was before their city, brought oxen and garlands unto the gates, and would have done sacrifice with the people. Which when the apostles, Barnabas and Paul, heard of, they rent their clothes, and ran in among the people, crying out, and saying, sirs, why do ye these things? We also are men of like passions with you, and preach unto you that ye should turn from these vanities unto the living God, which made heaven, and earth, and the sea, and all things that are there in:

> Who in times past suffered all nations to walk in their own ways. Nevertheless he left not himself without witness, in that he did good, and gave us rain from heaven, and fruitful seasons, filling our hearts with food and gladness. And with these sayings scarce restrained they the people, that they had not done sacrifice unto them."

Daniel made the mistake of allowing a man to worship him:

> (Dan. 2:46) "Then the king Nebuchadnezzar fell upon his face, and worshipped Daniel, and commanded that they should offer an oblation and sweet o'dours unto him."

Only Jesus gives forgiveness of sins:

> (Acts 5:31) "Him hath God exalted with his right hand to be a Prince and a Saviour, for to give repentance to Israel, and forgiveness of sins."

Only through Jesus is preached forgiveness of sin:

> (Acts 13:38) "Be it known unto you therefore, men and brethren, that through this man is preached unto you the forgiveness of sins."

Only redemption through the blood of Jesus is the forgiveness of sin:

(Eph. 1:7) "In whom we have redemption through his blood. The forgiveness of sins, according to the riches of his grace."

Only to Jesus are we to confess our sins. Because only He can forgive sins:

(1 John 1:9) "If we confess our sins, he is faithful and just to forgive us our sins, and to cleanse us from all unrighteousness."

Christians have no use for a human priest. All a priest would do for a Church Age Christian is hinder him. We have our High Priest, Jesus Christ:

(Heb. 3:1) "WHEREFORE, HOLY brethren, partakers of the heavenly calling, consider the Apostle and High Priest of our profession, Christ Jesus."

No man on earth can forgive sin or give blessings. This is according to scripture. Any man, be it a Pope, priest, or any other human who says he can is a liar:

(Rom. 3:4) "God forbid: Yea, let God be true, but every man a liar."

ORDINANCES

Our modern day ceremony is what could be classified as an ordinance. Since baptism and communion are the only two commandments given to a Church Age Christian that are ceremonies, we are to keep them:

> (1 Cor. 11:2) "Now I praise you, brethren, that ye remember me in all things, and keep the ordinances, as I delivered them to you."

Paul was given specific guidelines about communion. He received them from the Lord. Paul wasn't physically at the first communion but the Holy Spirit gave him instruction after his conversion:

> (1 Cor. 11:23) "For I have received of the Lord that which also I delivered unto you, That the Lord Jesus the same night in which he was betrayed took bread."

There are no commandments when or how often the Church is to set communion. It does command when it is taken you do it in remembrance of the Lord's death:

> (1 Cor. 11:24) "And when he had given thanks, he brake it, and said, Take, eat: this is my body, which is broken for you: this do in remembrance of me."

A Christian is to drink the grape juice and remember Christ's blood that was shed for us:

> (1 Cor. 11:25) "After the same manner also he took the cup, when he had supped, saying, This cup is the new testament in my blood: this do ye, as oft as ye drink it, in remembrance of me."

This cup is to have grape juice in it not fermented wine. It is supposed to be new wine:

> (Matt. 26:29) "But I say unto you, I will not drink henceforth of this fruit of the vine, until that day when I drink it new with you in my Father's kingdom."

This new wine is found in the cluster. In other words it isn't fermented. It is fresh juice or at least preserved, unfermented juice:

> (Isa. 65:8) "Thus saith the Lord, As the new wine is found in the cluster...."

Communion or the Lord's Supper is a memorial of the Lord's death. It is also a looking forward to His Second Coming. When the Christian takes the Lord's Supper he is to remember the Lord's death and look forward to His Second Coming.

> (1 Cor. 11:26) "for as often as ye eat this bread, and drink this cup, ye do shew the Lord's death till he come."

If a Christian takes communion unworthily he will be guilty of Christ's body and blood:

> (1 Cor. 11:27) "Wherefore whosoever shall eat this bread, and drink this cup of the Lord, unworthily, shall be guilty of the body and blood of the Lord."

There are two things that determine whether a man is guilty or unworthy. The first thing is does that person have any unconfessed sin in his life:

> (1 Cor. 11:28) "But let a man examine himself, and so let him eat of that bread, and drink of that cup."

The second thing is not discerning the Lord's body:

To discern the Lord's body is to know and believe that the people who have trusted Christ in this age are the Lord's body or the Church:

> (1 Cor. 12:12-14) "For as the body is one, and hath many members, and all the members of that one body, being many, are one body: so also is Christ. For by one Spirit are we all baptized into one body, whether we be Jews or Gentiles, whether we be bond or free; and have been all made to drink into one Spirit. For the body is not one member, but many."
> (1 Cor. 12:20) "But now are they many members, yet but one body."

If one does not discern the Lord's body or has any unconfessed sin in his life, he eats and drinks unworthily. He eats and drinks damnation or condemnation to himself. This is why some get sick and some sleep the sleep of death:

> (1 Cor. 11:30) "For this cause many are weak and sickly among you, and many sleep."

If we judge and confess our sin ourselves then Jesus Christ won't have to:

> (1 Cor. 11:31) "For if we judge ourselves, we should not be judged."

When Jesus Christ judges us, we will be punished so we won't be condemned with the world:

> (1 Cor. 11:32) "But when we are judged, we are chastened of the Lord, that we should not be condemned with the world."

When it is time to take communion, take it together. This is the best way to finish at the same time or to "tarry one for another."

> (1 Cor. 11:33) "Wherefore, my brethren, when ye come together to eat, tarry one for another."

If you are hungry eat at home or somewhere other than the communion table. If not the Church will be condemned together:

> (1 Cor. 11:34) "And if any man hunger, let him eat at home; that ye come not together unto condemnation. And the rest I will set in order when I come."

Come to the Lord's Supper knowing that the saved people in the Church Age make up the Lord's body. Come to the Lord's Supper with no unconfessed sin in your life. Come to the Lord's Supper remembering Jesus' death and looking forward to His return. Do not come to the Lord's Supper hungry. If you can't meet these scriptural qualifications you are better off to not take communion. Don't let the Pastor, time of communion, or anything else pressure you into taking the Lord's Supper unworthily. You will be the one judged not the person pressuring you. Remember it says eateth and drinketh damnation to himself (1 Cor. 11:29) it is personal.

The second ordinance in the Church Age we are to observe is baptism. Water baptism in the New Testament Church is a figure of the Spirit baptism that saves us. Water baptism will not save you and has nothing to do with the cleaning of the flesh. It is the answer, through the action of being immersed in water, of a good conscience toward God. The Spiritual baptism, that occurs at the time of salvation, is the one that saves by the resurrection of Jesus Christ (if Christ had not risen from death He would have been just like any other religious leader).

> (1 Pet. 3:21) "The like figure whereunto even baptism doth also now save us (not the putting away of the filth of the flesh, but the answer of a good consciece toward God,) by the resurrection of Jesus Christ."

Cornelius is a Gentile who prayed and was heard by God who told him to send to Joppa for Peter. Cornelius did so immediately and Peter came to him:

> (Acts 10:31-33) "And said, Cornelius, thy prayer is heard, and thine alms are had in remembrance in the sight of God. Send therefore to Joppa, and call hither Simon, whose surname is Peter; he is lodged in the house of one Simon a tanner by the sea side:

who, when he cometh, shall speak unto thee. Immediately therfore I sent to thee; and thou hast well done that thou art come. Now therefore are we all here present before God, to hear all things that are commanded thee of God."

Peter then preached the gospel to Cornelius and the other Gentiles:

(Acts 10:34) "Then Peter opened his mouth, and said, of a truth I perceive that God is no respecter of person."
(Acts 10:38-43) "How God anointed Jesus of Nazareth with the Holy Ghost and with power: who went about doing good, and healing all that were oppressed of the devil; for God was with him. And we are witnesses of all things which he did both in the land of the Jews, and in Jerusalem; whom they slew and hanged on a tree: Him God raised up the third day, and shewed him openly; Not to all the people, but unto witnesses chosen before of God, even to us, who did eat and drink with him after he rose from the dead. And he commanded us to preach unto the people, and to testify that it is he which was ordained of God to be the judge of quick and dead. To him give all the prophets witness, that through his name whosoever believeth in him shall receive remission of sins."

While Peter was preaching the Holy Ghost fell on the Gentiles that were listening. This means they were saved:

(Acts 10:44,45) "While Peter yet spake these words, the Holy Ghost fell on all them which heard the word. And they of the circumcision which believed were astonished, as many as came with Peter, because that on the Gentiles also was poured out the gift of the Holy Ghost."

Peter placed the water baptism after salvation. This is the correct order of things:

(Acts 10:47) "Can any man forbid water, that these should not be baptized, which have received the Holy Ghost as well as we?"

He then commanded that they be baptized in the name of the Lord.

(Acts 10:48) "And he commanded them to be baptized in the name of the Lord. Then prayed they him to tarry certain days."

Jesus commanded that all nations be baptized in the name of this Father, Son, and the Holy Ghost. He said "name" once signifying the three are one Lord. To baptize in the name of the Lord is to baptize in the name of the Father, Son and Holy Spirit. Jesus is Lord:

(1 Cor. 1:3) "Grace be unto you, and peace, from God our Father, and from the Lord Jesus Christ."

God the Father is Lord:

(Acts 2:34) "For David is not ascended into the heavens: but he saith himself. The Lord said unto my Lord, Sit thou on my right hand."

The Holy Spirit is Lord because He is co-equal and One with the Father and Jesus Christ:

(1 John 5:7) "For there are three that bear record in heaven, the Father, the Word, and the Holy Ghost: and these three are one."

In 1 Corinthians 10 it is clear that Gentiles in the Church Age are to be baptized in water after salvation. They are to be baptized in the name of the Father, Son, and Holy Ghost. Water baptism does not save a Christian in the Church Age, Spirit baptism does. After a person is born again and understands what water baptism is they should be baptized.

We are told to observe these ordinances. What happens if a person is saved and doesn't? To refuse to do what the Lord said to do is disobedience. Since a Church Age Christian can't go to hell he would probably be chastised. At the very least his growth spiritually would be stunted.

11. The Kingdom of God and the Kingdom of Heaven

The Kingdom of God and the Kingdom of Heaven are two completely different and separate kingdoms. The Kingdom of God is a spiritual kingdom:

> (Rom. 14:17) "For the kingdom of God is not meat and drink; but righteousness, and peace, and joy in the Holy Ghost."

The Kingdom of God is within you and you don't get it by looking for it:

> (Luke 17:20,21) "And when he was demanded of the Pharisees when the kingdom of God should come, he answered them and said, The kingdom of God cometh not with observation: Neither shall they say, Lo here! or, lo there! for, behold, the kingdom of God is within you."

The Kingdom of Heaven is strictly a physical kingdom:

> (Dan. 2:44) "And in the days of these kings shall the God of heaven set up a kingdom, which shall never be destroyed: and the kingdom shall not be left to other people, but it shall break in pieces and consume all these kingdoms, and it shall stand forever."

(Dan. 4:3) "How great are his signs! and how mighty are his wonders! his kingdom is an everlasting kingdom, and his dominion is from generation to generation."

(Dan. 4:34) "And at the end of the days I Nebuchadnezzar lifted up mine eyes unto heaven, and mine understanding returned unto me, and I blessed the most High, and I praised and honoured him that liveth forever, whose dominion is an everlasting dominion, and his kingdom is from generation to generation."

Satan was given these two kingdoms when he was created. He then lost them when iniquity was found in him:

(Eze. 28:15) "Thou was perfect in thy ways from the day that thou wast created, till iniquity was found in thee."

He was drawn away of his own lust and tempted to put his will above God's will:

(James 1:13-15) "Let no man say when he is tempted, I am tempted of God: for God cannot be tempted with evil, neither tempteth he any man: But every man is tempted, when he is drawn away of his own lust, and enticed. Then when lust hath conceived, it bringeth forth sin: and sin, when it is finished, bringeth forth death."

God could have prevented Satan from falling but He permits a lot of things to go on to work out His original plan:

> (Rom. 11:11) "I say then, Have they stumbled that they should fall? God forbid: but rather through their fall salvation is come unto the Gentiles, for to provoke them to jealousy."
>
> (Rom. 11:32) "For God hath concluded them all in unbelief, that he might have mercy upon all."

God then created Adam and gave him the two kingdoms. Adam had fellowship with God which is the spiritual kingdom:

> (Gen. 2:16,17) "And the Lord God commanded the man, saying, Of every tree of the garden thou mayest freely eat: But of the tree of knowledge of good and evil, thou shalt not eat of it: for in the day that thou eatest thereof thou shalt surely die."

God put man in a garden that had perfect conditions. This was the physical kingdom:

> (Gen. 2:8) "And the Lord God planted a garden eastward in Eden; and there he put the man whom he had formed."

Adam lived in the garden with his wife Eve. Adam lost both kingdoms when he was tempted by her and gave in. This is Adam's fall through which Adam lost both kingdoms:

(Gen. 3:12) "And the man said, The woman whom thou gavest to be with me, she gave me of the tree, and I did eat."

Eve was tempted by Satan and gave in to the temptation:

(Gen. 3:13) "And the Lord God said unto the woman, What is this that thou had done? And the woman said, The serpent beguiled me, and I did eat."

Through Adam's fall sin entered into the human race. When sin entered death followed. This sin was then passed to all people throughout time:

(Rom. 5:12) "Wherefore, as by one man sin entered into the world, and death by sin; and so death passed upon all men, for that all have sinned."

God is not responsible for Adam's or any other man's sin. He doesn't tempt any man:

(James 1:13) "For God cannot be tempted with evil, neither tempteth he any man."

After Adam's fall Satan then took over the physical kingdom again. He is still king over the physical earth. The difference now is the earth is under a curse:

(Eph. 2:2) "Wherein in time past ye walked according to the course of this world, according to the Prince of the power of the air, the spirit that now worketh in the children of disobedience."

The spiritual kingdom then went back to God. The Lord then gave the kingdoms to Noah. Noah then lost the kingdoms through disobedience. He got drunk and gave his son Ham the opportunity to sodomize him (which he did):

> (Gen. 9:20-24) "And Noah began to be an husbandman, and he planted a vineyard: And he drank of the wine, and was drunken; and he was uncovered within his tent. And Ham, the father of Canaan, saw the nakedness of his father, and told his two brethren without. And Shem and Japeth took a garment, and laid it upon both their shoulders, and went backward, and covered the nakedness of their father; and their faces were backward, and they saw not their fathers' nakedness. And Noah awoke from his wine, and knew what his younger son had done unto him."

The next person in line for a commission is Abraham. The Promise God made him is unconditional. It is for a piece of land on this earth:

> (Gen. 13:14,15) "And the Lord said unto Abram, after that Lot was separated from him, Lift up now thine eyes, and look from the place where thou art northward, and southward, and eastward, and westward: For all the land which thou seest, to thee will I give it, and to thy seed forever."

Abraham's descendants are then singled out to be the line from which the King emerges. Abraham has a son Isaac, Isaac has a son Jacob, and Jacob has a son Judah. Judah is the tribe that Jesus Christ comes through:

> (Heb. 7:14) "For it is evident that our Lord sprang out of Juda; of which tribe Moses spake nothing concerning priest hood."

It was prophesied that the King would be born of a virgin:

> (Isa. 7:14) "Therefore the Lord himself shall give you a sign; Behold, a virgin shall conceive, and bear a son, and shall call his name Immanuel."

Which came to pass exactly as prophesied:

> (Matt. 1:18) "Now the birth of Jesus Christ was on this wise: When as his mother Mary was espoused to Joseph, before they came together, she was found with child of the Holy Ghost."
> (Matt. 1:25) "And knew her not till she had brought forth her first born son: And he called his name Jesus."

Man falls and God bears the entire blame and redeems man:

> (Rom. 5:6) "For when we were yet without strength, in due time Christ died for the ungodly."

(Rom. 5:18,19) "Therefore as by the offence of one judgment came upon all men to condemnation; even so by the righteousness of one the free gift came upon all men unto justification of life. For as by one man's disobedience many were made sinners, so by the obedience of one shall many be made righteous."

Jesus Christ bears this blame by coming to earth as a man, passes the tempting of Satan, then dies on the cross:

(Matt. 4:1-11) "Then was Jesus led up of the Spirit into the wilderness to be tempted of the devil. And when he had fasted forty days and forty nights, he was afterward an hungered. And when the tempter came to him, he said, If thou be the Son of God, command that these stones be made bread. But he answered and said, It is written, man shall not live by bread alone, but by every word that proceedeth out of the mouth of God. Then the devil taketh him up into the holy city, and setteth him on a pinnacle of the temple, And saith unto him, If thou be the Son of God, cast thyself down: for it is written, He shall give his angels charge concerning thee: and in their hands they shall bear thee up, lest at any time thou dash thy foot against a stone. Jesus said unto him, It is written again, Thou shalt not tempt the Lord thy God. Again, the devil taketh him up into an exceeding high mountain, and sheweth him all the kingdoms of the world, and the glory of them; And saith unto him, All these things will I give thee, if thou wilt fall down and worship me. Then saith Jesus unto him, Get thee hence, Satan: for it is written, Thou shalt worship the Lord thy God, and him only shalt thou serve. Then the devil leaveth him, and, behold, angels came and ministered unto him."

(Rom. 5:10) "For if, when we were enemies, we were reconciled to God by the death of his Son, much more, being reconciled, we shall be saved by his life."

The guilt is all taken away from man and he will become a son of God which makes his soul sinless by receiving Jesus Christ as his Saviour:

(John 1:12,13) "But as many as received him, to them gave he power to become the sons of God, even to them that believe on his name: Which were born, not of blood, nor of the will of man, but of God."

God is just, man is unjust:

(1 Pet. 3:18) "For Christ also hath once suffered for sins, the just for the unjust, that he might bring us to God, being put to death in the flesh, but quickened by the Spirit."

In the person of Jesus Christ, God has a suitable person to whom to give the kingdoms. God goes as far as calling Him the last Adam:

(1 Cor. 15:45) "And so it is written, The first man Adam was made a living soul; the last Adam was made a quickening spirit."

John the Baptist and Jesus both said the Kingdom of Heaven is at hand:

(Matt. 3:2) "And saying, Repent ye: for the kingdom of heaven is at hand."
(Matt. 4:17) "From that time Jesus began to preach, and to say, Repent: for the kingdom of heaven is at hand."

Jesus said the Kingdom of God is at hand:

(Mark 1:15) "And saying, The time is fulfilled, and the kingdom of God is at hand: repent ye, and believe the gospel."

These two kingdoms are at hand in the person of Jesus Christ. Jesus is the King of Israel, who are the physical heirs:

(John 1:49) "Nathanael answered and said unto him, Rabbi, thou art the Son of God; thou art the King of Israel."

Jesus also had complete fellowship with God. This is the spiritual aspect:

(John 8:29) "And he that sent me is with me: the Father hath not left me alone; for I do always those things that please him."
(John 11:42) "And I knew that thou hearest me always: But because of the people which

stand by I said it, that they may believe that thou hast sent me."

The Kingdoms were ready to go into effect. They were "at hand." Then things changed and the Jews crucified the King:

(Matt. 27:35) "And they crucified him."

Jesus gave His life on the cross, was buried, and arose the third day:

(1 Cor. 15:3,4) "For I delivered unto you first of all that which I also received, how that Christ died for our sins according to the scriptures; And that he was buried, and that he rose again the third day according to the scriptures."

Then Stephen preached to the Jews who again had the opportunity to accept Jesus Christ as their Messiah. Again they rejected Him. It was to the point that Jesus was standing, ready to return:

(Acts 7:55,56) "But he, being full of the Holy Ghost, looked up stedfastly into heaven, and saw the glory of God, and Jesus standing on the right hand of God, And said, Behold, I see the heavens opened, and the Son of man standing on the right hand of God."

But they stoned Stephen and Jesus sat down:

> (Acts 7:59) "And they stoned Stephen, calling upon God, and saying, Lord Jesus, receive my spirit."
>
> (Col. 3:1) "If ye then be risen with Christ, seek those things which are above, where Christ sitteth on the right hand of God."

At this point in time God turned to the Gentiles and turned away from the Jews for some two thousand years. This is called the time of the Gentiles. The end of the time of the Gentiles is called the fullness of the Gentiles. The time of the Gentiles will span the Church Age, through the rapture and the Tribulation Period.

> (Rom. 11:25) "For I would not, brethren, that ye should be ignorant of this mystery, lest ye should be wise in your own conceits, that blindness in part is happened to Israel, until the fullness of the Gentiles be come in."

This time of the Gentiles will end at the Battle of Armageddon. This battle will be fought at Jesus Christ the King's return:

> (Rev. 11:2) "But the court which is without the temple leave out, and measure it not; for it is given unto the Gentiles: and the holy city shall they tread under foot forty and two months."
>
> (Rev. 16:15,16) "Behold, I come as a thief. Blessed is he that watcheth, and keepeth his garments, lest he walk naked, and they see his shame. And he gathered them together

into a place called in the Hebrew tongue Armageddon."

Upon Jesus Christ's return He will set up His Kingdom that will last forever:

(Dan. 2:44) "And in the days of these kings shall the God of heaven set up a kingdom, which shall never be destroyed: and the kingdom shall not be left to other people, but it shall break in pieces and consume all these kingdoms, and it shall stand forever."

The Kingdom of Heaven will last for one thousand years:

(Rev. 20:4) "And I saw thrones, and they sat upon them, and judgment was given unto them: and I saw the souls of them that were beheaded for the witness of Jesus, and for the word of God, and which had not worshipped the beast, neither his image, neither had received his mark upon their foreheads, or in their hands; and they lived and reigned with Christ a thousand years."

The Thousand Year or Millennial Reign will end in yet another confrontation called the battle of Gog and Magog:

(Rev. 20:8) "And shall go out to deceive the nations which are in the four quarters of the earth, Gog and Magog, to gather them together to battle: the number of whom is as the sand of the sea."

Characteristics of the Kingdom of Heaven:

The tempting of people won't be as it has been because Satan will be bound:

> (Rev. 20:2,3) "And he laid hold on the dragon, that old serpent, which is the Devil, and Satan, and bound him a thousand years, And cast him into the bottomless pit, and shut him up, and set a seal upon him, that he should deceive the nations no more, till the thousand years should be fulfilled: and after that he must be loosed a little season."

People will again live as long as they did in the days of Methuselah, if they aren't sinners:

> (Isa. 65:20) "There shall be no more thence an infant of days, nor an old man that hath not filled his days: for the child shall die an hundred years old; but the sinner being an hundred years old shall be accursed."
> (Gen. 5:27) "And all the days of Methuselah were nine hundred sixty and nine years: and he died."
> (Zech. 8:4) "Thus saith the Lord of hosts; There shall yet old men and old women dwell in the streets of Jerusalem, and every man with his staff in his hand for every age."

The light of the sun and moon will increase to seven times the level it is now:

> (Isa. 30:26) "Moreover the light of the moon shall be as the light of the sun, and the light of the sun shall be seven fold, as the light of seven days, in the day that the Lord bindeth up the breach of his people, and healeth the stroke of their wound."

There will be changes in the animal kingdom. The predators will stop eating meat and will live side by side with those animals formerly their prey. All the animals will eat grass. A little child will lead animals that were formerly dangerous. A child will be able to play with poisonous snakes without being harmed.

> (Isa. 11:6-9) "The wolf also shall dwell with the lamb, and the leopard shall lie down with the kid; and the calf and the young lion and the fatling together; and a little child shall lead them. And the cow and the bear shall feed; their young ones shall lie down together: and the lion shall eat straw like the ox. And the sucking child shall play on the hole of the asp, and the weaned child shall put his hand on the cockatrice' den. They shall not hurt nor destroy in all my holy mountain: for the earth shall be full of the knowledge of the Lord, as the waters cover the sea"

The earth will bring forth food in abundance:

> (Amos 9:13) "Behold, the days come, saith the Lord, that the plowman shall overtake the reaper, and the treader of grapes him that

soweth seed; and the mountains shall drop sweet wine, and all the hills shall melt."

Israel will be back in their land and will never again be moved:

(Amos 9:14,15) "And I will bring again the captivity of my people of Israel, and they shall build the waste cities, and inhabit them; and they shall plant vineyards, and drink the wine thereof; they shall also make gardens, and eat the fruit of them. And I will plant them upon their land, and they shall no more be pulled up out of their land which I have given them, saith the Lord thy God."

If any man prophesies his mother and father are to kill him:

(Zech. 13:3) "And it shall come to pass, that when any shall yet prophesy, then his father and his mother that begat him shall say unto him, Thou shalt not live; for thou speakest lies in the name of the Lord: and his father and his mother that begat him shall thrust him through when he prophesieth."

There will be a pilgrimage every year of the nations of the earth to come to Jerusalem to worship the King. Jesus Christ will sit on the throne of David to receive the worship. If these people don't come there will be drought. If the family of Egypt doesn't go up after the rain has been withheld they will be smitten by the plague (it is a certain plague which is probably leprosy) if they don't come to keep the feast of tabernacles:

(Zech. 14:17,18) "And it shall be that whoso will not come up of all the families of the earth unto Jerusalem to worship the King, the Lord of hosts, even upon them shall be no rain. And if the family of Egypt go not up, and come not, that have no rain; there shall be the plague, where with the Lord will smite the heathen that come not up to keep the feast of tabernacles."

The desert will blossom like a rose. There won't be any sickness. Water will be abundant. A highway will be there called the way of holiness that no unclean person will be permitted on. All sorrow and sighing will be gone. Those bought by the blood of Christ will return to Zion with peace and singing:

(Isa. 35:1-10) "The wilderness and the solitary place shall be glad for them; and the desert shall rejoice, and blossom as the rose. It shall blossom abundantly, and rejoice even with joy and singing: the glory of Lebanon shall be given unto it, the excellency of Carmel and Sharon, they shall see the glory of the Lord, and the excellency of our God. Strengthen ye the weak hands, and confirm the feeble knees. Say to them that are of a fearful heart, be strong, fear not: behold, your God will come with vengeance, even God with a recompence; he will come and save you. Then the eyes of the blind shall be opened, and the ears of the deaf shall be unstopped. Then shall the lame man leap as an hart, and the tongue of the dumb sing: for in the wilderness shall waters break out, and streams in the desert. And the parched ground shall become a pool, and the thirsty land springs of water: in the habitation of dragons, where each lay, shall be grass with reeds and rushes and an highway shall be there, and a way, and it shall be called The way of holiness; the unclean shall not pass over it; but it shall be for those: the wayfaring men, though fools, shall not err therein. No lion shall be there, nor any ravenous beast shall go up thereon, it shall not be found there; but the redeemed shall walk there: And the ransomed of the Lord shall return, and come to Zion with songs and everlasting joy upon their heads: they shall obtain joy and gladness, and sorrow and sighing shall flee away."

THE SERMON ON THE MOUNT

Matthew chapters five, six, and seven have been used for all manner of false doctrine. This is done by applying them falsely to the Church. Remember this is doctrine for the Millennial Reign. This is the "constitution" for the Kingdom of Heaven. Consider examples of difference between the Church Age and Millennial Reign:

A person in the Church Age that is meek is run over. They inherit the earth in the Kingdom of Heaven:

(Matt. 5:5) "Blessed are the meek: for they shall inherit the earth."

A Church Age Christian has no worry at all about going to hell for calling someone a fool. One in the Millennial Reign can go to hell for this. contrast the section on eternal security to:

> (Matt. 5:22) "But I say unto you, That whosoever is angry with his brother without a cause shall be in danger of the judgment and whosoever shall say to his brother, Raca, shall be in danger of council: but whosoever shall say, Thou fool, shall be in danger of hell fire."

It makes no difference in the Church Age how many body parts a Christian cuts off as far as going to hell is concerned. But in the Millennial Reign circumstances are different. Contrast the section on eternal security to:

> (Matt. 5:29,30) "And if thy right eye offend thee, pluck it out and cast it from thee: for it is profitable for thee that one of thy members should perish, and not that thy whole body should be cast into hell. And if thy right hand offend thee, cut it off, and cast it from thee: for it is profitable for thee that one of thy members should perish, and not that thy whole body should be cast into hell."

Regardless of what a Church Age Christian does he is forgiven of past, present, and future sins. In the Millennial Reign you have to forgive to receive forgiveness. Contrast the section on eternal security also:

> (Matt. 6:14,15) "For if ye forgive men their trespasses, your heavenly Father will also forgive you: But if ye forgive not men their trespasses, neither will your Father forgive your trespasses."

A person in the Millennial Reign is forbidden to judge anyone. In the Church Age you are told to judge all things if you are spiritual:

> (Matt. 7:1) "Judge not, that ye be not judged."
> (1 Cor. 2:15) "But he that is spiritual judgeth all things, yet he himself is judged of no man."

ABOUT THE KINGDOM OF GOD:

People who do not believe the Scriptural doctrine of eternal security will attempt to persuade others that Gal. 5:19-21 proves a Christian can lose his salvation. The Kingdom of God is spiritual, exists inside the believer, and has the characteristics of joy, peace, and righteousness in the Holy Ghost. If you do the works of the flesh after salvation you will not inherit the Kingdom of God. This is not to say you will lose your salvation. What it is saying is you will not inherit or possess while you are here on earth righteousness, peace, and joy in the Holy Ghost. In other words: if you do the works of the flesh, you will be out of fellowship with Jesus Christ and miserable:

> (Gal. 5:19-21) "Now the works of the flesh are manifest, which are these; Adultery, fornication, uncleanness, lasciviousness,

Idolatry, witchcraft, hatred, variance, emulations, wrath, strife, seditions, heresies, Envyings, murders, drunkenness, revellings, and such like: of the which I tell you before, as I have also told you in time past, that they which do such things shall not inherit the kingdom of God."

The Kingdom of Heaven and Kingdom of God are absolutely not the same. One is physical and one is spiritual. For someone to make them the same is to hide the trail of Satan throughout the history of man and create a doctrinal catastrophe.

12. Daniel's Seventy Weeks

Looking into the future the next item on God's calendar is the Rapture or calling out of the church:

> (Rev. 4:1) "After this I looked, and, behold, a door was opened in heaven: and the first voice which I heard was as it were of a trumpet talking with me; which said, come up hither, and I will shew thee things which must be hereafter."

As of now, for over two thousand years God has not dealt with Israel as a nation, He allowed the Jews to become blind in part to the fact that Jesus was their Messiah. This period of time is still going on and will last until God is finished dealing with Gentiles:

> (Rom. 11:25) "For I would not, brethren, that ye should be ignorant of this mystery, lest ye should be wise in your own conceits, that blindness in part is happened to Israel, until the fullness of the Gentiles be come in."

Once God has raptured the Church and finishes with the Gentiles, in the Tribulation Period, He will save Israel as a nation and take away her sins:

> (Rom. 11:26,27) "And so all Israel shall be saved: as it is written, there shall come out

of Sion the Deliverer, and shall turn away ungodliness from Jacob: For this is my covenant unto them, when I shall take away their sins."

God gave Daniel this prophesy which gives a time element and some detail concerning what this time period will accomplish: He said seventy weeks are determined or will be carried out against "thy people," or the Jews. The seventy weeks will settle things between God and Israel. It will finish the transgression of Israel's disobedience to God. It will make an end of sins for Israel. It will make reconciliation for Israel's iniquity. It will bring in everlasting righteousness for Israel. It will seal up or insure the vision or prophecy. It will anoint the most Holy, who is Jesus Christ:

> (Dan. 9:24) "Seventy weeks are determined upon thy people and upon thy holy city, to finish the transgression, and to make an end of sins, and to make reconciliation for iniquity, and to bring in everlasting righteousness, and to seal up the vision and prophecy, and to anoint the most Holy."

The seventy weeks spoken of in Daniel cannot be four hundred ninety literal days. This fact is affirmed when it is determined that the command to restore and build Jerusalem came to Nehemiah under the rule of King Artaxerxes 446 B.C.:

> (Neh. 2:1) "And it came to pass in the month Nisan, in the twentieth year of Artaxerxes the king, that wine was before him: and I took up the wine, and gave it unto the king,

now I had not been before time sad in his presence."

(Neh. 2:5,6) "And I said unto the king, if it please the king, and if thy servant have found favour in thy sight, that thou wouldest send me unto Judah, unto the city of my fathers' sepulchres, that I may build it. And the king said unto me, (the queen also sitting by him,) for how long shall thy journey be? And when wilt thou return? So it pleased the king to send me; and I set him a time."

From the time of the command to build Jerusalem until the time that the Messiah was cut off or Christ was crucified was sixty-nine weeks:

(Dan. 9:25,26) "Know therefore and understand, that from the going forth of the commandment to restore and to build Jerusalem unto the Messiah the Prince, shall be seven weeks, and threescore and two weeks: the street shall be built again, and the wall, even in troublous times. And after threescore and two weeks shall Messiah be cut off, but not for himself: and the people of the prince that shall come shall destroy the city and the sanctuary; and the end thereof shall be with a flood, and unto the end of the war desolations are determined."

The command to build Jerusalem was given in 446 B.C. Jesus Christ was cut off or crucified in 29 A.D. By having this information we know that the seventy weeks are not literally 490 days. Since scripture informs us of what happens on both these dates we know that it is literally 490 years. Daniel 9:26 says after sixty-nine weeks or 483 years the Messiah will be cut off or crucified. At the crucifixion of Christ the seventy weeks stopped, hereby leaving one week or seven years remaining. This seven year period that remains will begin after the rapture of the Church. This last seven year period is Daniel's Seventieth Week or the Great Tribulation Period:

> (Gen. 29:20) "And Jacob served seven years for Rachel; and they seemed unto him but a few days, for the love he had to her."
> (Gen. 29:27,28) "Fulfill her week, and we will give thee this also for the service which thou shalt serve with me yet seven other years. And Jacob did so, and fulfilled her week: and he gave him Rachel his daughter to wife also."

Something that needs to be taken into consideration is the years between 446 B.C. and 29 A.D. add up to only 475 years by the worldly calendar of 365 days. If you multiply 475 years by 365 days you get 173,375 days. Since God's calendar consists of 360 days (which will be proven by the Scripture that follows) you then divide 173,375 days by 360 days. This gives an answer of 481 years and 145 days. This is reconciled to be 483 years by counting parts of years, leap years, and what discrepancy that occurs between man's calendar and God's calendar. Genesis tells us the time of the flood is one hundred fifty days from the seventeenth day of the second month to the seventeenth day of the seventh month. This means each month has thirty days and each year three hundred sixty days:

> (Gen. 7:24) "And the waters prevailed upon the earth an hundred and fifty days."

> (Gen. 7:11) "In the six hundreth year of Noah's life, in the second month, the seventeenth day of the month, the same day were all the fountains of the great deep broken up, and the windows of heaven were opened."
>
> (Gen. 8:3,4) "And the waters returned from off the earth continually: and after the end of the hundred and fifty days the waters were abated. And the ark rested in the seventh month, on the seventeenth day of the month, upon the mountains of Ararat."

It is made known to us that the Tribulation Period will last seven years by this account. Most every other scripture concerning the Great Tribulation speaks in terms of two three and one-half year time periods. These periods are broken down into time (one year), times (two years), and dividing of time (one-half year):

> (Dan. 7:25) "And he shall speak great words against the most High, and shall wear out the saints of the most High, and think to change times and laws: and they shall be given into his hand until a time and times and the dividing of time."
>
> (Rev. 12:14) "And to the woman were given two wings of a great eagle, that she might fly into the wilderness, into her place, where she is nourished for a time, and times, and half a time, from the face of the serpent."

There will rise up a wicked prince, which is the antichrist, who will make a covenant with the Jews for this seven year period. In the middle or midst of the seven years he will stop the Jews from offering sacrifices or making oblations to God in the temple. The overspreading of the abomination of desolation will go on until the end of the Great Tribulation.

> (Dan. 9:27) "And he shall confirm the covenant with many for one week: and in the midst of the week he shall cause the sacrifice and the oblation to cease, and for the overspreading of abominations he shall make it desolate, even until the consummation, and that determined shall be poured upon the desolated."

Jesus spoke of this abomination of desolation:

> (Matt. 24:15) "When ye therefore shall see the abomination of desolation, spoken by Daniel the prophet, stand in the holy place, (whoso readeth, let him understand)."

This abomination will be the antichrist physically walking into the temple, claiming to be God and doing all sorts of filthy acts:

> (2 Thes. 2:4) "Who opposeth and exalteth himself above all that is called God, or that is worshipped; so that he as God sitteth in the temple of God, shewing himself that he is God."

Chapters 5 to 19 in the Book of Revelation deals with the happenings of this seventieth week of Daniel as does Matthew 24 and 25. Daniel Chapter 9 covers this seven year period as does several other passages in the Old

Testament. Job is a picture of the Jews being persecuted then restored. Job has forty-two chapters as the last half of the Tribulation has forty-two months or three and one half years.

Again sixty-nine of the seventy weeks or 483 of the 490 years have already taken place. Two thousand years of the Church Age have passed since God stopped the progression of the seventy weeks. The Church Age separates Daniel's sixty-ninth and seventieth weeks. This seventieth week will produce the salvation of Israel, bring back the signs, and salvation by faith and works:

> (1 Cor. 1:22) "For the Jews require a sign, and the Greeks seek after wisdom."
> (Rev. 12:17) "And the dragon was wroth with the woman, and went to make war with the remnant of her seed, which keep the commandments of God, and have the testimony of Jesus Christ."
> (Rev. 14:12) "Here is the patience of the saints: here are they that keep the commandments of God, and the faith of Jesus."

This should be enough information to give the Christian a general understanding of Daniel's Seventieth Week. For a detailed explanation get Clarence Larkin's Commentary on the Book of Daniel.

13. John's and Peter's Baptisms

John the Baptist came baptizing Jews to ready them for Jesus Christ's First Coming. John's baptism has nothing to do with a Church Age Christian. No, the Baptists of today cannot be traced back to John the Baptists. The reason being is a Church Age Christian would have to go back under the Law, submit to baptism by a Jew who isn't preaching grace through faith but water baptism unto repentance. John's baptism was not a picture or figure of the death, burial, and resurrection of Jesus Christ. It is a picture of the sinner dying and being buried knowing he had to face God's wrath at death and acknowledging that Jesus Christ had to come and take his place.

John came baptizing people in water:

> (Matt. 3:11) "I indeed baptize you with water unto repentance: but he that cometh after me is mightier than I, whose shoes I am not worthy to bear: he shall baptize you with the Holy Ghost, and with fire."
> (Mark 1:8) "I indeed have baptized you with water: but he shall baptize you with the Holy Ghost."
> (Luke 3:16) "John answered, saying unto them all, I indeed baptize you with water."

The reason John came baptizing in water was to make Jesus Christ manifest to Israel:

> (John 1:31) "And I knew him not: but that he should be made manifest to Israel, therefore am I come baptizing with water."

Since John's baptism was to make Christ manifest to Israel, all those who submitted to John's baptism were made aware by God that Jesus was the Christ:

> (Matt. 16:17) "And Jesus answered and said unto him, blessed art thou, Simon Bar-Jona: for flesh and blood hath not revealed it unto thee, but my Father which is in heaven."

John the Baptist came and baptized with water so people would know who Jesus Christ was. In other words when the Jews would believe John's message and submit to his water baptism God would open their spiritual eyes and reveal Jesus Christ to them as their Messiah.

The Apostle Peter's baptism was to manifest Jesus Christ to Israel before the crucifixion. Peter's baptism is after the crucifixion. Why then did Peter tell these people to be baptized? Before this question can be answered there needs to be some scriptural background laid:

Peter was preaching to the men of Judaea and those who dwell at Jerusalem:

> (Acts 2:14) "But Peter, standing up with the eleven, lifted up his voice, and said unto them, Ye men of Judaea, and all ye that dwell at Jerusalem, be this known unto you, and hearken to my words."

Peter was preaching to the men of Israel telling them of Jesus Christ who did miracles, wonders, and signs before them showing He was approved of God:

> (Acts 2:22) "Ye men of Israel, hear these words; Jesus of Nazareth, a man approved of God among you by miracles and wonders and signs, which God did by him in the midst of you, as ye yourselves also know."

Peter told them Christ was crucified by wicked hands, by the determinate counsel, and the foreknowledge of God:

> (Acts 2:23) "Him, being delivered by the determinate counsel and foreknowledge of God, ye have taken, and by wicked hands have crucified and slain."

Peter quoted David speaking of the resurrection of Christ:

> (Acts 2:31,32) "He seeing this before spake of the resurrection of Christ, that his soul was not left in hell, neither his flesh did see corruption. This Jesus hath God raised up, whereof we all are witnesses."

Peter told these men of Israel that God has made Jesus both Lord and Christ:

> (Acts 2:36) "Therefore let all the house of Israel know assuredly, that God hath made

that same Jesus, whom ye have crucified, both Lord and Christ."

Having now some background in the scripture as to what was happening just prior to Peter's baptism we can scripturally understand it. These people were pricked in their hearts or they were so sorry they hurt in their hearts. This is when the question was asked "what shall we do?" They didn't ask what they should do to be saved but what should they do in view of the fact that they crucified the Christ:

> (Acts 2:37) "Now when they heard this, they were pricked in their heart, and said unto Peter and to the rest of the apostles, men and brethren, what shall we do?"

Peter then told them what to do. He said to repent and be baptized in the name of Jesus Christ for the remission of sins. This word "for" is the same as because of. In other words he was telling them to repent (turn away from) and be baptized in Jesus Christ's name because your sins are remitted upon the belief of what Peter was telling them. He then told them when they were baptized they would receive the Holy Ghost:

> (Acts 2:38) "Then Peter said unto them, Repent, and be baptized everyone of you in the name of Jesus Christ for the remission of sins, and ye shall receive the gift of the Holy Ghost."

Again, Acts is a transitional book. It moves from Law to Grace. There is a major doctrinal difference between what Peter is saying here and how Paul told a Church Age Christian to get saved."

> (Eph. 2:8,9) "For by grace are ye saved through faith; and that not of yourselves: it is the gift of God: Not of works, lest any man should boast."

For a Church Age Christian salvation is the gift of God. So what would happen to a lost person in the Church Age if they would repent and be baptized? The answer is they would still die and go to hell. It wouldn't matter how many times the lost would repent and be baptized because to repent and be baptized is works. You cannot work for salvation in the Church Age. Nothing could be clearer.

Furthermore you do not get the Holy Ghost in the Church Age by repenting and being baptized. You get the Holy Ghost in the Church Age by trusting in Christ. You are Spiritually baptized by the Holy Spirit into the Body of Christ by receiving Jesus Christ:

> (1 Cor. 12:13) "For by one Spirit are we all baptized into one body, whether we be Jews or Gentiles, whether we be bond or free; and have been all made to drink into one Spirit."

In the Church Age no type of water baptism will do anything for anyone who is lost. John's baptism and Peter's baptism both are works being performed in transitional periods. The doctrines of these transitional periods have nothing to do with a Christian. If a person rightly divides (2 Tim. 2:15) he will know this. Don't let anyone fool you into thinking that either of these two baptisms are for a Church Age Christian, it is nonsense.

14. The Great White Throne Judgment

The Great White Throne Judgment is the last judgment before eternity. It is the judgment that most people speak of or profess to know of. There are different ideas of what will take place at this judgment, but the Bible is specific about it. Let us see what God's Word has to say about this matter.

Time and eternity will be peeled back to reveal a great white throne. On this throne sits the Ancient of Days or God Almighty.

> (Rev. 20:11) "And I saw a great white throne, and him that sat on it, from whose face the earth and heaven fled away; and there was found no place for them."
>
> (Dan. 7:9,10) "I beheld till the thrones were cast down, and the Ancient of Days did sit, whose garment was white as snow, and the hair of his head like the pure wool: his throne was like the fiery flame, and his wheels as burning fire. A fiery stream issued and came forth from before him: thousand thousands ministered unto him, and ten thousand times ten thousand stood before him: the judgment was set, and the books were opened."

All the unsaved dead will stand before God. Their position in life, wealth, or acquaintances will carry no weight. Whether a powerful king or a drunk wallowing in the gutter, if they died lost they will be here. There will be books opened and all lost people will be judged out of the books by their works. The books probably refer to the Bible. It has books in it and it didn't say their works will be written in the books. Man has never committed a sin that is not recorded in the King James Bible. The book of life will be opened which contains the names of the saved.

> (Rev. 20:12) "And I saw the dead, small and great, stand before God; and the books were opened: and another book was opened, which is the book of life: and the dead were judged out of those things which were written in the books, according to their works."
>
> (John 12:48) "He that rejecteth me, and receiveth not my words, hath one that judgeth him: the word that I have spoken, the same shall judge him in the last day."

The sea will give up the dead which are the fallen angels that drowned in Noah's flood (1 Pet. 3:19,20). These angels had given up their first estate (Jude 6) which was spiritual. These angels then put on flesh and cohabitated with human women (Gen. 6:2). Hell will give up it's dead which is the unsaved of all ages. Death will give up its dead which are the saved from the Great Tribulation and Millennial Reign.

> (Rev. 20:13) "And the sea gave up the dead which were in it: and death and hell delivered up the dead which were in them:

and they were judged every man according to their works."

(1 Pet. 3:19,20) "By which also he went and preached unto the spirits in prison; which sometime were disobedient, when once the longsuffering of God waited in the days of Noah, while the ark was a preparing, wherein few that is, eight souls were saved by water."

(Jude 6) "And the angels which kept not their first estate, but left their own habitation, he hath reserved in everlasting chains under darkness unto the judgment of the great day."

(Gen. 6:2) "That the sons of God saw the daughters of men that they were fair; and they took them wives of all which they chose."

Death here is the same place that Jesus called Paradise and Abraham's bosom.

(Luke 23:43) "And Jesus said unto him, Verily I say unto thee, To day shalt thou be with me in paradise."

(Luke 16:22) "And it came to pass, that the beggar died, and was carried by the angels into Abraham's bosom: the rich man also died, and was buried."

In the Old Testament, Paradise was the place the saints went at death and rested until Jesus Christ died on the cross and led them to heaven.

(Eph. 4:8) "Wherefore he saith, When he ascended upon high, he led captivity captive, and gave gifts unto men."

Paradise was and will be in the center of the earth across a divider or great gulf from hell. No inhabitant of hell or Paradise can cross this divider. They have to stay where they are placed.

(Luke 16:23-26) "And in hell he lift up his eyes, being in torments, and seeth Abraham afar off, and Lazarus in his bosom, And he cried and said, Father Abraham, have mercy on me, and send Lazarus, that he may dip the tip of his finger in water, and cool my tongue; for I am tormented in this flame. But Abraham said, Son, remember that thou in thy lifetime receivedst thy good things, and likewise Lazarus evil things: but now he is comforted, and thou art tormented. And beside all this, between us and you there is a great gulf fixed: so that they which would pass from hence to you cannot; neither can they pass to us, that would come from thence."

During the Great Tribulation and Millennial Reign God will use Paradise to temporarily hold the saints of those two ages. Then at the time of the Great White Throne Judgment these saints along with the unsaved dead and fallen angels will be brought in front of the throne and judged (Rev. 20:13).

Since there will be time no more, there will be no more use for hell or Paradise. With no more use for these temporary places of the dead, they will be cast into the lake of fire.

> (Rev. 20:14) "And death and hell were cast into the lake of fire. This is the second death."
>
> (Rev. 10:6) "And sware by him that liveth for ever and ever, who created heaven, and the things that therein are, and the earth, and the things that therein are, and the sea, and the things which are therein, that there should be time no longer."

The lake of fire is burning with brimstone or sulfur.

> (Rev. 19:20) "These both were cast alive into a lake of fire burning with brimstone."

The unsaved will have their part and will be placed into the lake of fire. The Bible calls this the second death.

> (Rev. 21:8) "But the fearful, and unbelieving, and the abominable, and murderers, and whoremongers, and sorcerers, and idolaters, and all liars, shall have their part in the lake which burneth with fire and brimstone: which is the second death."

The saved outside of the Church Age will be judged here:

> (Rev. 11:18) "And the nations were angry, and thy wrath is come, and the time of the dead, that they should be judged, and that

thou shouldest give reward unto thy servants the prophets, and to the saints, and them that fear thy name, small and great; and shouldest destroy them which destroy the earth."

Just as sure as the new heavens, new earth, and New Jerusalem are eternal so is the lake of fire. Anyone not written in the book of life will have to pay for their sins. When you sin against an Eternal God you will pay for that sin eternally. There is no getting out of the lake of fire. Once there, you burn forever and are never consumed.

15. Conclusion

Through the course of this book we have studied a number of different doctrinal matters. You have been shown how to rightly divide by dispensations. Any other method of study will cause you to "wrongly divide" and cause huge doctrinal problems. All the heresies taught in the Church Age are done by applying doctrine given to a dispensation other than the Grace Age and trying to apply it to the Church. This not only causes confusion but it causes those teaching false doctrine to lead others astray. God is not the author of this mess (1 Cor. 14:33). By not applying these verses "rightly" you teach salvation by works, baptism, speaking in tongues and any number of ways to get to heaven other than the blood of Jesus Christ.

You are saved by grace through faith, not works. You get this salvation by trusting that the sacrifice that Jesus Christ made on the cross, or the shedding of His sinless, perfect blood will pay for your sins. Once you accept Him as your Saviour you are saved forever, regardless of what works your flesh does or does not do. Therefore the fear of hell is gone and you can work for Jesus.

If you are saved you should be working for the Lord. If you have not trusted Jesus Christ for the saving of your soul you are lost. As it stands you are headed for hell. The good news is it doesn't have to end this way. You have a choice. It can be heaven instead of hell, God instead of Satan, and eternal life instead of eternal punishment. Choose Jesus Christ today and you choose eternal life.

Index

A

Abraham 10, 16, 17, 18, 37, 104, 105, 134, 135
Adam 1, 2, 3, 5, 7, 8, 102, 103, 107, 108
Antichrist 33, 71, 85, 86, 87, 124, 125

B

Baptism .... vii, 45, 46, 47, 48, 54, 68, 92, 96, 98, 99, 127, 128, 130, 131, 138

C

Christian ...... vii, xi, 25, 27, 29, 37, 38, 40, 42, 43, 44, 47, 50, 53, 54, 55, 56, 57, 58, 59, 60, 64, 70, 72, 73, 78, 81, 91, 92, 93, 94, 99, 116, 117, 118, 126, 127, 131
Church.. v, vi, vii, viii, 24, 25, 26, 27, 28, 29, 30, 32, 37, 38, 40, 42, 43, 44, 45, 46, 47, 49, 50, 52, 53, 54, 56, 58, 60, 61, 64, 65, 70, 72, 73, 74, 75, 76, 77, 81, 82, 83, 86, 87, 88, 91, 92, 94, 95, 96, 99, 110, 116, 117, 118, 120, 123, 126, 127, 131, 136, 138
Church Agevii, 25, 29, 37, 38, 40, 42, 43, 44, 45, 47, 49, 50, 52, 53, 54, 56, 60, 61, 64, 70, 72, 73, 81, 88, 91, 92, 96, 99, 110, 116, 117, 118, 126, 127, 131, 136, 138
Communion 92, 93, 94, 95, 96

D

David 22, 23, 35, 52, 99, 114, 129
Dispensation... ix, 1, 5, 10, 15, 21, 23, 26, 30, 33, 34, 36, 37, 38, 40, 45, 51, 52, 138
Division .... x, 86
Doctrine .... vi, vii, viii, x, 24, 25, 38, 40, 43, 44, 45, 53, 60, 61, 116, 118, 138

E

Eternal Security 39, 52, 53, 56, 81, 117, 118
Eve 1, 2, 3, 5, 7, 102, 103

F

Faith .ix, x, 12, 17, 22, 25, 26, 27, 29, 32, 35, 41, 42, 46, 47, 49, 50, 51, 52, 54, 61, 64, 65, 66, 126, 127, 131, 138

G

Gentile 38, 63, 72, 96
Grace .x, 12, 17, 22, 24, 25, 26, 27, 38, 49, 50, 52, 61, 67, 89, 91, 99, 127, 130, 131, 138
Great White Throne Judgment 132, 135

H

Healing .... vi, vii, 20, 24, 62, 63, 64, 66, 97
Holy Ghost/Spirit .viii, x, 2, 6, 12, 17, 22, 27, 28, 32, 35, 45, 46, 47, 48, 49, 50, 54, 55, 59, 68, 69, 92, 97, 98, 99, 100, 105, 109, 118, 127, 130, 131

I

Israel .... vii, 15, 17, 19, 20, 21, 22, 23, 24, 28, 29, 30, 32, 33, 38, 41, 44, 62, 63, 71, 84, 90, 108, 110, 114, 120, 121, 126, 127, 128, 129

J

Jesus Christ ... v, x, 21, 23, 26, 27, 30, 31, 37, 38, 41, 46, 47, 48, 49, 50, 52, 56, 58, 59, 61, 63, 64, 65, 69, 72, 75, 76, 77, 79, 81, 82, 83, 84, 91, 95, 96, 99, 105, 106, 107, 108, 109, 110, 111, 114, 118, 121, 122, 126, 127, 128, 129, 130, 131, 134, 138
Jew 22, 38, 44, 62, 63, 72, 127

K

Kingdom of God 100, 108, 118, 119
Kingdom of Heaven 40, 100, 108, 111, 116, 119

L

Law .... xi, 15, 21, 24, 37, 41, 45, 47, 50, 51, 56, 127, 130

M

Millennium 24, 34
Moses 19, 20, 26, 62, 63, 105
Mystery 32, 71, 73, 82, 83, 84, 86, 87, 88, 110, 120

N

New Birth .... vii, 2, 6, 12, 17, 22, 27, 32, 35, 38
Noah 5, 8, 9, 10, 13, 104, 124, 133, 134

P

Priest .... vii, 88, 90, 91, 105

R

Rapture 26, 30, 58, 73, 75, 83, 88, 110, 120, 123
rightly divide .... vi, viii, ix, 41, 45, 68, 131, 138
Rightly Divide 43
Roman/Rome 28, 30, 86
Rome 86

S

Salvation .... vii, ix, x, 2, 6, 12, 17, 22, 25, 27, 28, 29, 32, 35, 39, 41, 46, 47, 48,
 49, 50, 51, 52, 53, 54, 55, 56, 60, 61, 75, 76, 77, 81, 83, 96, 98, 99, 102,
 118, 126, 131, 138
Saved.. v, vii, x, xi, 25, 26, 27, 29, 32, 39, 41, 42, 44, 46, 47, 48, 49, 50, 51, 52,
 53, 54, 55, 58, 59, 60, 63, 75, 78, 81, 83, 84, 96, 98, 99, 107, 120, 130, 131,
 133, 134, 136, 138
Seventy Weeks 22, 120, 121, 122, 126
Signs ...... vi, vii, 23, 33, 39, 44, 62, 63, 64, 65, 70, 71, 72, 87, 88, 101, 126, 129

T

Tongues .... vi, vii, 24, 39, 49, 62, 63, 64, 67, 68, 69, 70, 138
Transition 24, 29, 38, 40, 44
Tribulation .... vii, 24, 29, 33, 40, 41, 42, 44, 45, 51, 60, 61, 71, 75, 76, 80, 84,
 110, 120, 123, 124, 125, 126, 133, 135

W

Works..x, 2, 6, 22, 25, 28, 29, 31, 32, 35, 41, 47, 49, 50, 51, 52, 54, 55, 61, 65, 66, 77, 78, 81, 118, 126, 131, 133, 138